From Stuck
to Unstuck

overcoming congregational impasse

Kenneth A. Halstead

An Alban Institute Publication

Scripture quotations, unless otherwise noted, are from the New Revised
Standard Version of the Bible, copyright © 1989, Division of Christian
Education of the National Council of the Churches of Christ in the
United States of America, and are used by permission.

Library of Congress Catalog Card Number 98-73667
ISBN 1-56699-203-6

CONTENTS

ACKNOWLEDGMENTS

I would like to thank my teachers in family therapy, especially Herbert Anderson, Connie Salts, and Anthony Heath; my CPE supervisor, Preston Bogia; and my family therapist, William Proctor, all of whom played major roles in opening my eyes to the concepts in this book. I am grateful to Harris Lee for reading an earlier manuscript and encouraging my efforts to write. I would like to thank my colleagues in campus and parish ministry, especially those in my local text study, for providing stories, encouraging me, and letting me bounce these ideas off them. I thank Connie for many hours of typing rough drafts and for comments on parts of the text. I thank Peter Steinke for offering useful and challenging critique on the manuscript. I thank my editors, especially Beth Gaede, who provided encouragement and constructive suggestions to me as a new writer. Finally, I thank the members of various congregations and others too numerous to mention who shared stories, frustrations, ideas, and encouragement.

ACKNOWLEDGMENTS

Free the Flow, Fan the Flame

Oh, to feel the love of God flowing like living water through our congregation. Oh, that the Holy Spirit would lead us to experience healing and new energy for service and witness! The trouble is, not everyone wants the congregation to be a versatile and seaworthy ship piloted toward mission through choppy seas by a bold, dynamic crew. Some people look to the parish for an anchor of predictability. For them, risk and creativity offer more threat than joy.

Where We Are

Most of us probably stand somewhere between these poles when we think about change in the church. We want more life and love in our churches, but we fear what change might mean for us; or we are skeptical that change is possible. The struggle arises not only between two kinds of people but also between the congregation's need for stability and its need for change. Achieving a balance is difficult even when change is relatively slow. The situation becomes increasingly complicated when change feels like a rumbling earthquake beneath our feet.

To make matters worse, we do foolish things in our anxiety to achieve balance. We in the church often behave like sailors hanging their weight out opposite sides of a sailboat to steady it. The more one group leans to the port side, the more others must compensate by leaning to starboard. The result may be a semblance of stability, if all keep doing their part, but much effort is wasted, and the ship loses the agility to make turns and adjustments. Meanwhile, waves kick up, prompting even more panicky attempts to keep the balance.

I cannot prescribe a single formula to achieve balance or sail the ship. The needed wisdom and resources may reside within your church already, if you can just release and access them. But often we become stuck: The more we try to solve problems, the worse they get.

- One group tries to solve a congregation's conflict by determining who is to blame, but blame polarizes and results in more elusive hidden conflict.
- A preacher, attempting to shame a congregation into action, further undermines cooperation.
- An administrative leader seeks solutions through more elaborate structure. In the process spontaneity is stifled, and members are demoralized.
- Leaders address their efforts at change to the formal leaders and organization of the congregation. The result is a structure opposed by many because it seems to devalue the informal structure and leadership.

Demand brings rebellion. Pursuit leads to flight. Superrational argument meets emotional resistance.

Such attempted solutions may be automatic reactions or well-rationalized beliefs. They may spring from good intentions and may seem to have worked in the past. We therefore tend to believe that we are doing the right thing and that any other course of action would be wrong, even crazy (for example, that facing a conflict or opening up a secret could profoundly hurt or destroy a congregation). Consequently, when the solution fails, instead of trying a whole new strategy, we try more of the same. Things get worse, and the cycle continues. The feedback from our strategy either automatically triggers a repetition through unconscious emotional reactions, or we misread the feedback and, with apparent rationality, do more of the same. Either way, things get worse until we are stuck in a more-of-the-same maze and cannot find our way out.

In our congregations our behaviors, beliefs, and feelings in reaction to each other, as in the examples above, serve as reinforcing feedback in a spiraling loop, creating more intense or more rigid problems. This book is concerned mainly with the things we do (or avoid doing) in our congregations to solve emotional issues—conflict, anger, anxiety, hurt, fear, jealousy, frustration, confusion. What we do, especially in response to emotions, can determine whether the love- and life-giving energy of God is loosed or blocked by our attempts to make things better.

My hope is that stuck congregations (and the larger structures of which they are a part) may begin to see their repeated patterns of failure in trying to solve systemic emotional problems, that they may avoid doing more of the same, and that they may try something different in a spirit of experimentation born of faith in a gracious God.

I know something about stuck groups, the ways group members get stuck individually and corporately, and some clues to getting unstuck. I believe this knowledge can be helpful to many "stuck" congregations. Using the approach this book describes, for example, people in a congregation I will call St. Paul's broke out of an old pattern of trying to solve stewardship problems and created an unorthodox approach that unleashed more generosity in giving than they had dreamed possible. Members of St. Mark's, stuck in a series of conflicts, identified the subtle destructiveness of their usual methods and found a new approach that brought a healing that endured.

The Perspective of Experience

I have experienced and observed the failures and the pain of pastoral leadership. Along with many small successes and satisfactions, I have gotten stuck more than a few times and experienced a generous dose of pain in pastoral work. I have also counseled many pastors and members about the painful experiences in their churches.

My numerous contacts over the past decade with young adults and those who work with young adults have been a wake-up call for me. These encounters have sensitized me to the depth and scope of the challenge the church faces. They have convinced me that many congregations have buried their heads in the sand about what is happening to their youth and young adults and the radical changes needed in how we "do church."

It is evident to me as a campus pastor that superficial changes—throwing in a little contemporary worship or hiring a youth worker—will not suffice. Much of the church cannot be taken seriously by the majority of young adults. It is stuck in overlearned solutions supported by an old worldview that is far too passive, superficial, narrow, rigid, boring, removed from reality, and oblivious to the pain and paradoxes of growing up today.

Of course, segments of this young adult population are turning to traditionalist worship and moderated-for-market fundamentalism. From such religion they get a sense of clarity and security amid a churning and changing world. We must take seriously their need for stability and a credible structure. But the longer-term message to the church is that we must change our ways profoundly. We must adapt our ways of "doing church" so that all of us, including these young people, can hear and experience the creative, life-giving power of the gospel. If we try to force them into the mold of yesterday's church, we will continue to lose them. As a campus pastor I feel compelled to sound the trumpet about what is at stake—not only for the faith of our youth, but also for the future of the institutional church.

Training in family therapy and in systems theory has helped me to keep my sanity in highly stressful situations and to dig myself and the groups I lead out when we find ourselves mired in reactive emotional muck. This training has also helped convert me to what I call the new paradigm. I have changed the way I see and experience these phenomena:

- The nature of reality (from mechanistic, reductionistic, and static to organic, holistic, and dynamic).
- The way we know and make meaning (from logic, objectivity, certainty, and separation from what is known to an emphasis on story, knowing within a context, accepting that our knowledge is approximate, and participating with what is known).
- Our relationship to nature (from conquest, domination, prediction, and competition to harmony, partnership, mystery, and cooperation).
- Our understanding of self (from extreme individualism, body/mind split, and self as machine or computer to individual accountable to community, body/mind unity, and self as organism).

This concept of "paradigm" strikes more deeply at the philosophical roots and more broadly at the implications of this shift than other common usages of the term. It suggests that to be faithful to our mission in a changing world, we must change our thinking about the way we think, our approach to problem-solving, and virtually everything else we do in the church. Our worldview, our overarching paradigm, must shift to allow us to make these important adaptations and to solve the complex problems we face. We are moving from a view of reality as isolated, static, and understandable by dissection or analysis to seeing reality as interrelated, dynamic wholes related to *the* whole, understood only through respectful, loving participation. God is at work in this paradigm shift, and God can use it to help us be more faithful and credible in our mission.

A Focused, Limited Role

In the roles of family therapist and of pastor, I usually operate within the perspective of the so-called Brief Family Therapies. This approach offers in many ways a humbler vision than that usually conjured up by the word therapy. It tends to generalize to all kinds of problem-solving in all kinds of groups. In this approach, leaders play a focused and limited role. Trying to solve all of the group's problems or to be its savior would be viewed as reinforcing one of the most common attempted solutions that gets congregations stuck: looking for a rescuer instead of taking responsibility and creating solutions together.

According to Brief Family Therapies, leaders get the system unstuck so that health-giving and growth-giving forces flow free. Then the group can move on to solving its own problems, coping with its insolvable difficulties, and discerning which are which. Once they are unstuck, emotional systems like families and congregations have a tremendous capacity for love, flexibility, and creativity.

After each step of progress, leaders will anticipate fallbacks and stuck points and seek to nurture changes that can continue to grow until they gradually displace old patterns. I refer to these two aspects of leadership in stuck situations as (a) "freeing the flow" and (b) "fanning the flame." Leaders and helpers do not do the healing or solve the problems by themselves. They help the group get unstuck. Then they get out of the way so that God's creative energies can flow through it more fully.

The role of leaders is not so much to generate energy as to remove blocks and unleash bound-up energy and health. God is at work in the group before leaders enter the scene, and God will continue working after they are gone. In Mark 4:26-29 Jesus compares the dominion of God to a farmer who planted seeds and then went on with daily life, sleeping and waking. The miraculous growth was God's doing. The parable implies that we have a role in planting and harvesting, but the rest of our task is mainly to wait and to watch as God gives the growth, and to be surprised by the bountiful yield. The church leader's role is to free the flow of God's growth forces and to feed the sparks of the Spirit's life-giving energies so that they may become a steady and sustained flame.

I do not propose this method as a total philosophy of church leadership adequate to every situation. Leadership involves a complex of roles, and leaders must relate to a host of subsystems within and to larger systems beyond the congregation. However, if a leader does not deal effectively with certain stuck points in the system and its subsystems (such as with ongoing internal power struggles or secrets blocking communication), and free up their inherent energies, he or she is unlikely to lead the church successfully. One can work with administrative might and ingenuity on budget, buildings, programs, and publicity, but if one does not find a way to help change overlearned emotional solutions that create problems, growth will be obstructed or limited in all these areas.

There are reasons to focus our role on "merely" freeing the flow and fanning the flame. First, most pastors and lay leaders are not trained and under supervision as therapists. Nor should we use this book to convince ourselves that we can quickly become amateur therapists or systems experts. However, I hope leaders will be encouraged to get together and humbly ask what patterns of stuckness we face and what we could do differently. I hope readers will be challenged by reading this book to examine their assumptions and encouraged to risk new approaches within the limits of freeing the flow and fanning the flame.

A second reason for choosing a focused and limited role is that people's experience of time has changed. Pastors and congregational leaders must realize that we have less time than we once had to make a difference for people. Like those less willing to wait for therapy to work and to listen to long, boring sermons, many are less willing to give the congregation much time to prove itself. Unless we are focused enough to make a relatively quick and significant difference in their lives, they will turn elsewhere. We are called to share the word and the fruits of our faith in a fast-changing, impatient world. The limits on a leader's time call for a special kind of focus—efficient interventions at key points in the process that can help us make a difference quickly.

Systemic Brief Therapy models[1] were designed to solve people's problems as efficiently as possible, preferably in only a few sessions, usually by actively intervening and building on strengths. These therapies do not try to bring about internal growth or profound insight in individuals or to overhaul entire family systems. They simply get people's lives unstuck and back to some degree of normality so that clients can solve their own problems. Applied to church leadership, some of the ideas from the Brief Systemic Therapies can help us accept a limited yet significant role, and they can help us achieve the maximum benefit possible, given the time constraints.

I will draw primarily on the approach of the Mental Research Institute (MRI) in Palo Alto, California. This approach, which maintains that our attempted solutions often create problems and that true solutions often require paradoxical interventions, fits well with my theological viewpoint, which keys on two themes: (a) the problems we create—sin, alienation, brokenness, stuckness—by our efforts to "save" ourselves and establish self-righteousness (our attempted solution) and (b) the paradoxical "solution" of salvation by grace alone.

Stuckness as Gift?

This Brief Therapy approach helps us bring about change without being perfect. It encourages a gracious and humane spirit of playful experimentation. Some versions of therapy commended for pastors and lay leaders seem to suggest that if we know enough we can stay in control (at least of ourselves) and avoid getting stuck emotionally in systems where we try to help. However, it can be a dangerous and discouraging half-truth to suggest that staying unstuck is the norm for competent therapists, pastors, and leaders. Those who are highly competent simply tend to admit sooner that they are stuck, get the help they need, and make the most of the situation when they have blown it.

The most freeing and powerful insight I have gained from family therapy for pastoral ministry rests on the belief that besides all the life-stealing forces, a creative, personal, life-giving growth force, which we believers call God, works despite and often precisely *through* our stuck points and failings.

The heart of my theology is this: We are saved by grace through faith once and for all and day by day. We do not grow more perfect in the usual sense. At best, we may become more aware of our sins and imperfections and our dependence on God's grace. We may grow more humble, grateful, gracious, compassionate, and able to laugh at ourselves—and thus more truly human. Still, we continue to make mistakes, to sin, and to get stuck spiritually and emotionally. Indeed, God seems to use precisely our failures, our pain, our struggles, and our little experiences of death to bring about growth.

We as leaders are called to make use of our painful stuck points and those of our members. Skilled therapists use awareness of their own emotional processes, including feeling stuck, as a radar to help them assess what is happening in the therapy session. The feelings of being stuck help us pinpoint the important issues for the counselor and counselees and to work for a breakthrough.

But despite our grasp of theory and the skills we possess, systemic therapy will never suffice to keep us on top of everything. Emotional systems are too complicated and fast-moving. The likelihood of getting stuck emotionally may be greater for most pastors and church leaders than for professional counselors because of the complexity of congregational emotional systems, our lack of training in how emotional systems work, and our assumptions about how people will behave in congregations.

All of us will most likely get stuck many times when we come to the important, potentially transformative growth issues between us and those with whom we work. The good news is that we are not condemned or proved incompetent by getting emotionally stuck. We are given an opportunity, through a little death and rebirth, to make a leap of growth and offer a significant resource to the groups we lead.

Church as Learning Organization

One more reason suggests itself for using the Brief Therapy approach: Knowing that we will sometimes get emotionally stuck can help us stay humble and flexible—much-needed qualities in times of rapid change.

Individuals and organizations need to learn and adapt to stay faithful to their mission. In addition, society today places a high value on flexibility, responding to customer feedback, and adapting or "reinventing" organizational structures and norms. Professor and best-selling business author Peter Senge says businesses must become "learning organizations."[2] So too must congregations and the large organizations of which they are a part. Institutions stuck in their ways will not likely remain credible to many. They may not survive long. Brief Therapies can help churches prepare for future mission.

I do not suggest that congregational leaders should try to become amateur therapists or pretend to be systems experts after reading this book. No one should presume to play such a role without specialized training and ongoing supervision. In one respect, however, the only qualification leaders need to use this book well is to know when they feel stuck and to possess the humility to know they need to do something different.

Such prerequisites do not require specialized training. Leaders can mutually share the frustrations they encounter in particular relationships or in seeking to bring about positive change for the larger group. They can use this book to help them discern the patterns of attempted solution which they use repetitively and which do not seem to be working. They can brainstorm and encourage one another to take risks and experiment to find responses that express a different pattern. I believe ordinary leaders can use the concepts and tools in this book to help them apply a different way of thinking—one that is counterintuitive and fun and that opens up options and strategies not previously considered.

Parts of this book are demanding, especially the early chapters. I trust that readers will be patient and persistent. Perhaps you will bite off just one chapter at a time and use the discussion questions to help digest it. We are covering relatively new territory for many. By virtue of our central point (doing something different), the map I lay out contravenes what some would consider common sense, and that fact makes for difficult reading. In addition, I am asking readers to think in a manner contrary to the way most of us tend to think in Western society. I do not believe you need to be a therapist to make good use of the techniques I describe. Probably we are already using some of these techniques in our congregations and in our daily life.

What I hope to do is help you to identify the methods you use, to learn new ones, and to use them all in ethical and responsible ways.

Ultimately their responsible use will depend on the maturity and wisdom of those who use them. Please use this book and related resources carefully to hone your wisdom and maturity in how you use these techniques.

Change and Leadership

This book seeks to provide a way for pastors and other leaders to work together to get themselves emotionally unstuck and to help their congregations as systems get unstuck. Because many of our smaller problems are a product of the current paradigm shift, this book strives also to use ideas about problem-solving from Brief Systemic Therapy to shed light on the implications of this paradigm shift for our communities of faith. It urges our leaders to anticipate the birth of churches and synagogues that reflect the new paradigm and to guide us to learn the role of midwife.

This book first asks: What is the nature of systemic problems in which we get stuck? And then: What is the nature of the solutions that get us unstuck? The other key question: What is the nature of leadership for our times that can best help us get our churches unstuck while keeping leaders emotionally healthy?

Illustrations are drawn from my own experiences and observations and from the stories of others. I do not contend that they are perfectly objective. I share them for three reasons. First, I want to illustrate the situation that puts many pastors and congregations in jeopardy. Second, I want to suggest theologically sound and practical steps to foster greater sanity and renewal. Third, I hope to get leaders talking with one another about emotional stuckness, brainstorming how to get free, and drawing on vision- and hope-stimulating stories about times when God's creative love has flowed through the congregation and how sparks of that love might be nurtured and fanned into flames for mission.

The biases and limitations of my social location will be obvious to many who read this book. I have made no attempt to hide the fact that I am a Lutheran Christian and a white, middle-class male. I have served primarily small rural congregations and campus ministry groups, and I have conducted some family therapy and systems-oriented workshops on the side. I am enthusiastic about what family therapy can teach the leaders of religious communities, however, and I believe that much of this book can be useful beyond my own circles to the wider religious community.

CHAPTER 1

What Is Stuckness?

Old Cornerstone Church has plenty of money, but it seems stuck in conflict. Even after members got rid of the people they thought were the problem and clarified authority lines and job descriptions, new troublemakers appeared, stepping into the same role. New signs of anger and discontent arose, leading to more dissension. Are these problems unrelated, or are they symptoms of underlying processes in the church's emotional system?

Sacred Cross Church was once known for its spiritual vitality, exciting worship, and loving atmosphere. Over time these qualities have faded, and longtime members talk about missing the spirit of their old church. Members have long believed that strong pastoral leadership, combined with pious, unquestioning acceptance of that leadership, was important to their church's success. If the right pastor were chosen and if members followed his lead, the old spirit would return. But they have seen a succession of pastors with a variety of gifts, and still renewal has not taken root. Are these concerns the result of people expecting too much of their church and pastor, or could it be that this church has gotten systemically stuck? Could it be that in these changed times, old structures and solutions that once worked can no longer foster the hoped-for spirit?

Some Definitions

For now we need to get some handles on systems and on this slippery concept of systemic stuckness. Admittedly, the term "stuck" is subjective and probably impossible to prove in a given situation. Nonetheless,

I believe the word points to an experience many people have had and to phenomena that often occur in systems. People experience it when their congregation does not seem to hear and respond to needs, is unable to foster a maturing faith in its members, and is unable to grow and adapt its structure to change. Such a congregation frustrates many members and feels as if it is going nowhere or losing ground. Its energy flow stagnates or drains away.

In contrast, people in an unstuck congregation experience:

- An energizing effect from participating in and talking about their congregation.
- Open communication with few restrictions on what can be talked about.
- Confidence that leaders, fellow members, and the organization as a whole listen and respond to needs.
- A sense of growing as a group toward maturity and greater faithfulness.
- Effective adaptation to a changing world.

While there are many ways to explain such phenomena, I believe malfunctioning behavioral feedback loops need to be corrected to allow people and systems to listen, respond, and adapt to each other to meet needs more effectively. *Feedback* is information received *in response* to information sent. Feedback that continually modifies and feeds on itself forms a feedback loop. People and events are not explained by simple cause and effect—one person causing another to feel a certain way. People affect each other in a circular fashion. What I do and feel affects what you do and feel, which then affects what I do and feel, and so on in a continuous loop that has no single starting or ending point. Such loops are part of larger loops and are woven throughout our relationships. Feedback loops, circles, or cycles are the heart of systems.

I use the term *system* to refer to *a group of people or parts that is organized by the consistent interrelationship of the parts, so that what happens with each part affects the others, and the whole takes on an identity that is more than the sum of its parts. This whole regulates itself through feedback loops both internally and in relation to the external environment.*

Human systems have many levels, from formal organizational levels to informal levels of emotional organization. All levels involve and affect emotions to some degree. The more long-term commitment members have to one another and to the group, the larger and more consistent is the role played by emotional feedback loops—interactions in which emotions like anxiety, anger, joy, and affection feed off each other. Congregations, like families, tend to develop such commitment, and thus emotional feedback loops often play an enormous role in their life.

If we can identify some of these loops and map how they are working, we can devise strategies to interrupt destructive loops and encourage creative ones. Sometimes a simple intervention—for example, a staff support committee helping a pastor respond nondefensively to criticism—can interrupt the "vicious circle" of criticism, defensiveness, more convinced criticism, more angry defense or withdrawal, more people drawn into criticizing, more people drawn into defending the pastor, more intense criticism, and so on. At other times an intervention as simple as a few leaders encouraging the pastor to notice and accept love and affirmation and return it to the congregation can foster a creative feedback loop. Such a "virtuous circle" can be self-reinforcing and build on itself to shape a wonderful, mutually encouraging partnership.

Feedback loops exist not only between individuals but also between and among the many levels of subsystems in a system, and between that system and the external environment. The concept of system organization or structure, which many systems thinkers use, can help us visualize some of these interrelationships. For example, systems like a congregation are organized or structured both formally and informally, and the two structures are not necessarily the same. In fact, many of the systemic muddles that keep us stuck arise when formal and informal structures (like elected leaders or written operating procedures, on the one hand, and the unelected, emotional leaders to whom other members defer, or customary ways of operating, on the other hand) contradict or work against each other. The resulting contradiction may confuse everyone and prevent change. Or, when it escalates, the feedback between these two systemic levels may create a painful "noise" analogous to microphone feedback.

"Rules" is another word family therapists use in talking about the system structure or feedback loops. Rules include implicit norms, explicit values, and the feedback mechanisms a system uses to enforce them. Rules can be formally stated but often are implicit. Again, rules can qualify or contradict each other, as when a congregation holds the explicit value of openness and honesty but punishes openness by gossiping critically about or excluding a member who talks freely about feelings.

I use the term "solutions" to refer to ingrained ideas and habits about how to solve problems. But more broadly, I use the term to include implicit solutions—ideas and habits—expressed in the feedback loops, the structure and rules of a system by which it organizes itself and seeks to solve the difficulties involved in people's living and working together.

It is the thesis of this book that stuckness is not primarily the result of stubborn or bad people, or even of lack of technique or of faulty formal structure. Rather *stuckness is primarily the result of well-intended attempted solutions built into the rules and structure of the system— solutions that create life-draining feedback loops.*

Such loops may produce so much stability that the system cannot adapt to change, as when a divided congregation is stalemated by two conflicting visions never consciously acknowledged and articulated. The factions bicker over minor issues to distract from the larger and more threatening vision issue, but they balance each other out so that nothing changes. Each time feedback begins to bring the vision issue into awareness, a symptom arises to distract attention, functioning to balance what could otherwise become escalating anxiety or conflict. Sometimes these symptoms are escalating feedback loops in the small picture but are part of a de-escalating loop in the larger system. Such can be observed in a family where a child acts out and draws the parents' anger toward himself, distracting them from a marital argument that threatened to escalate.

Another example: An associate pastor at the all-white Emmaus Tabernacle began asking the senior pastor and the board of deacons how the tabernacle could be located so near a black neighborhood and yet have no black members. Anxiety began to escalate. At the same time, an argument was heating up between the pastors over the associate's failure to keep office hours. After a prolonged fight, the associate was forced to resign. The race issue was dropped, and things returned to "normal." A less-threatening escalating loop served to distract from another, more threatening one and functioned to de-escalate the latter. Thus the group avoided the race issue (and remained stuck in its avoidance).

Destructive feedback loops may also involve behaviors that mutually escalate like an arms race, as in a congregation when one faction becomes angry and the other becomes even more angry. The more extreme action one group takes, the more extreme action the other takes, until hurt and anger are deep and widespread.

The concept of stuckness includes conscious attempts at a solution that make things worse. More significantly, stuckness points to the destructive feedback loops (both de-escalating and escalating or reinforcing) that result from attempted solutions implicit in the structure or rules of the system.

Essentially, stuckness is trying to solve difficulties of living and working together in community in ways (usually the same old ways) that make things worse by creating self-reinforcing, vicious circles. The problem may get worse right away (when a fight escalates) or seem to improve at first and get worse later (when we try to cover up and ignore pain, only to experience symptoms of repressed pain later). In either case, when things get worse, more of the original solution is tried, and the cycle continues.

Feelings of frustration and futility can be important signals of stuckness, but the feelings may say more about ourselves than about our congregation. Members may feel that their congregation is on the move, but they may in fact be stuck in misguided enthusiasm that fosters spiritual pride and self-serving injustice or ignorance. The congregation may be growing at the expense of excluding the voices of some ethnic, gender, or age group. In other cases, a leader may feel frustrated and believe the congregation is stuck when in reality it is growing slowly and doing low-profile mission, unnoticed and unappreciated by the leader. Feelings alone do not clarify the location of stuckness or its resolution. We need to step back, look at behavioral feedback loops, and try to discern if they are functioning in a way that helps the congregation grow and adapt faithfully.

Evil, Disease, or Stuckness?

Before we go any further, it is important to discuss why I use the term "stuckness" instead of relying on such words as sin, evil, and disease. Stuckness could, in many cases, be attributed to sin or evil on the one hand, or to emotional disease on the other. Sin, evil, and disease are important words. Sometimes the church will remain stuck until it calls sin "sin," evil "evil," and disease "disease," and takes appropriate action. My choice of the metaphor of stuckness is not accidental. The concepts of sin, evil, and disease are often used in an individualistic, mechanical, and oversimplified manner. Too often these words are used to demonize our opponents and blind us to our own sins.

The metaphor of "stuckness" lends itself to a systems understanding that looks at how the whole group works together, for better or worse. It points to pragmatic action we can pursue together without wasting time and energy on blame or shame. Until we learn to interpret sin, evil, and disease more systemically, the concept of stuckness may simply be more widely useful. It implies that God is already at work but that we are blocking God's creative love; that our task is not to try harder but to get out of the Spirit's way and encourage rather than quench the Spirit's working in our midst.

Why Spin Our Wheels?

Some congregations are stuck in ways so painful or obvious that they cannot deny their condition. These congregations may be ready to act, but they do the wrong thing. Leaders, and perhaps members, feel as if the whole group is stuck in the mud. The more they try to get unstuck, the faster the wheels spin and the deeper the hole is dug. They may believe they can get themselves out of the hole if they keep spinning their wheels, or if they soup up the engine so the wheels spin faster. This futile activity can continue for years before leaders or members try backing up or calling for help to push or pull them out.

These congregations remind me of a friend who wanted to be an engineer but kept failing calculus, a prerequisite for engineering school. His pride and determination led him to repeat calculus five times, each time thinking he could pass the course by trying harder. The sixth time he took a different tack, previously unthinkable. He humbled himself and hired a tutor, who helped him approach problems and learning in a new way. The result? He aced his final, passed the course with a B-plus, and was accepted into engineering school. To this day, he tells me that willingness to seek help is one of the most useful lessons he ever learned, for engineering and for life in general. He was willing not only to get help but also to break out of the pattern and try something different.

The temptation to spin our wheels, to try to solve problems with old solutions, is probably greater for groups like congregations. They play out repeated interactions and power struggles that amplify or bury their anxiety, "complexify" the situation by entangling more people, and justify their pride and behavior through systemic rules, myths, and beliefs. These group dynamics ensure that the old unworkable solutions become even more rooted. We do more of the same (such as talking behind the scenes, assigning another committee, intellectualizing, looking for a new pastor to rescue us, or avoiding conflict at all costs), even when it does not work, because these strategies have worked so well for us in many situations. In *Understanding Your Church as a System*, Leas and Parsons, noted experts on church conflict, say that the seeds of our stuckness are hidden in our past successes (or what we believe to have been successes.)[1] Because certain strategies seem to work so well, we overlearn them, overgeneralize them, overapply them, and become stuck.

We may even become addicted to them, as we see dramatically illustrated in the case of alcohol and other drug addictions. Drugs like alcohol are reliable in their effects and "work" for people in a variety of ways. They ease social anxiety and relieve tension, and alleviate mental pain. They provide an excuse for immature behavior and resolve the dilemma of how to rebel against constraints and feel independent without growing up and facing adult responsibilities. Using alcohol as a solution often leads to much bigger problems for the individual and for society. Alcohol may then be used in an attempt to cope with the new problems its abuse has created. In this way, a stuck, self-reinforcing cycle develops. The more alcohol is used as a solution, the more we believe we need it. The cycle gets overlearned and difficult to break for individuals, family, and society.

We overlearn and overgeneralize solutions also because family, close reference groups, and the broader culture tell us these are the right solutions. These strategies become entrenched in the stories, beliefs, "habits of the heart," rules, roles, rituals, and loyalties of families, institutions, and cultures. When overlearned solutions are woven into our communal way of life, it is no simple matter to change them. Sometimes overlearned solutions stick with us because they do make us feel better in the short run, even though they create bigger problems for us down the road. Two overlearned solutions are conflict suppression and scapegoating. A common example is conflict successfully suppressed ("solved") for a time but not finished. It simmers underground, surfacing and erupting again months or years later. The same thing occurs when a pastor is successfully scapegoated for some problem and moves away, so that neither congregation nor pastor has to examine and change systemic arrangements and habits. A few years later the same sort of problem may appear for the congregation or for the former pastor.

Lack of Awareness

Another part of our stuckness is simple lack of awareness. We do not get a handle on the smaller self-reinforcing cycles in which we are involved and see how they fit into the larger picture. In our highly individualistic culture, we tend to believe that we need to break things down into smaller pieces to understand and manipulate them and that we can then put them back together like a machine. It is difficult for us to see interactional processes and systemic wholes. We tend to notice isolated pieces of reality. Emotional systems are complex, and we lose sight of them when our focus is on individuals or isolated parts of the picture. Think, for example, how difficult it is to sort out fairly who did what when two children get in a fight, let alone when many people interact over a longer period.

Systemic processes have to do primarily with the "in between and among" of relationships and not just the pieces in isolation. But it is difficult for us to get a handle even on the most important pieces of our emotional systems, the self-reinforcing cycles in which we are directly involved (whether they are virtuous and life-giving or vicious and destructive). These cycles are difficult for us to see, partly because it is so difficult to see ourselves as others see us. So we tend to notice others' part and not our own in a self-reinforcing cycle, and to attribute good intentions to ourselves and less noble intentions to our adversaries. It does not occur to us to question our problem-solving efforts and the effects we are having.

Self-reinforcing cycles are hard to see also because we notice results that occur close in time to behaviors and conclude, often wrongly, that there is an immediate cause-and-effect relationship. In reality, there may have been many influences that brought about the result; some of the most important influences may have occurred long before.

Sometimes it is difficult to recognize the stuckness of our congregations because we are so used to this state of affairs. For example, if you grow up in a church where you always feel guilt and shame after worship, you may assume that church is supposed to be that way. You may even begin to cherish those feelings and protect them if they are associated with other feelings of security and continuity.

We may also be aware of symptoms like shame, secrecy, boredom, or conflict and want to change them but not be aware how our attempts to solve or heal these symptoms (such as avoiding conflict or getting defensive about our shame) feed and sustain them, and may themselves have become the bigger problem. Failing to see how our attempted solutions create the symptoms, we may address the symptoms by trying harder and doing more of the same, simply making the problem bigger and more stuck.

What makes matters more difficult is our lack of well-developed language, even in the church, for holistic realities and their subtleties (e.g., soul, spirit, process, meaning). We rarely see and make meaning of that for which we lack words. The complexity and "non-thingness" of emotional systems, combined with the lack of words and the dynamics of pride, fear, and misguided love, all make it unlikely that a typical group of congregational leaders will be able to see what is going on systemically, let alone lift themselves out of a systemic problem by their own bootstraps.

Handles and Levers

Understanding the stuckness of an entire congregation can be a daunting task. Stuckness can occur with individuals, marriages, and families, congregational subgroups of any size (boards or committees or the pastor and one or more members), whole congregations, and larger institutional and cultural systems (denomination, town, country, etc.). Stuckness can occur at any level and in any aspect of organizations from interpersonal relations to finances and mission outreach.

Fortunately, one need not handle an entire stuck system at once to start getting things unstuck. Usually an effective start can be made by getting a handle on smaller problems. Stuckness at one level is usually paralleled or complemented by stuckness at interconnected levels of the system. A smaller instance may serve as a metaphor for larger processes and may even be a lever for change. It is no small matter if two leaders with emotionally significant roles in a congregation become reconciled or break out of an impasse, or if the governing board breaks out of negativism and learns to brainstorm playfully. Assuming they stay in touch with other people and groups who play a key emotional role in the congregation and do not get sucked back into the old unspoken emotional "rules" for how things must be done, the change could reverberate throughout the congregation's emotional system and beyond.

I visualize the connection between the smaller problems and the stuckness of a whole congregation in the metaphor of the church as a body. A body is an organic, systemic whole in which all parts are interrelated. The body is system made up of subsystems—including the circulatory, respiratory, neural, and immune systems. When one part hurts, the whole body hurts. When one part gets stuck or clogged up, the whole system is affected. Smaller stuck points that clog up one of the body's subsystems affect the whole. When this subsystem gets unclogged and its processes begin to flow freely, other bodily subsystems may begin to clear up. Soon the health of the whole body is improved.

Every emotional system gets stuck at times. The stuckness can vary in intensity and complexity. Sometimes specialized outside help must be sought. I suspect that all congregations have at least some parts that are getting sticky at any given time. Sometimes it is mainly the pastor or a few leaders who feel the stuckness. To help a system get unstuck, it is generally most practical to start with oneself. If you feel stuck or believe your congregation is stuck, first take a long look at your own behavior and ask how it may feed into the behavior of others ("first take the log out of your own eye..." [Matt. 7:5]).

Questions

1. In what ways is the emotional life of your church stuck? What role are you playing in keeping things stuck?

2. How might your church be blocking the flow of God's Spirit by the way it deals with emotions and tries to solve problems?

3. Why isn't just trying harder enough to get an emotional system unstuck?

4. What are some of your church's favorite overlearned solutions?

5. What small relational or problem-solving change might have the most reverberations throughout your church? How can you help make this happen?

CHAPTER 2

Is Your Congregation Stuck?

Determining whether a congregation is stuck is less a matter of establishing fact than of discerning if using the label will help you get unstuck together. The family therapy movement, from which I draw many approaches, is suspicious of labels, especially those that pathologize or demonize. Such labels often ignore a problem's subtle systemic aspects, contribute to scapegoating, and aggravate stuckness. As a label, "stuckness" points to situations in which problem-solving efforts seem not to lead to real solutions but to make things worse. It can be a useful label because it guides us away from blame, focuses on good intentions gone awry, and points toward surprising ways to break through an impasse.

How are stuckness, pathology, sin, and evil related? I would like to keep these concepts distinct. In many cases, it is most helpful to avoid referring to stuckness as sick, sinful, or evil. But stuckness always involves some degree of what psychiatrists would call pathology and what theologians would call sin. I visualize stuckness on a continuum involving increasing degrees of complexity and sometimes an increasing degree of three factors involved in sin and evil:

- Denial or deceit
- Bondage, entrapment or oppression
- Malicious destructiveness

Denial, oppression, and destruction also occur in pathology but without the malicious intent to deceive, enslave, and destroy.

Each of these terms builds on different metaphors, a different kind of language, and a different perspective to describe problems. They may describe the same situation in different ways.

It is difficult to identify the point at which stuckness becomes pathological or evil. The term "evil" implies a direct and pervasive involvement of human will and, perhaps, a higher satanic will to dominate and destroy, and responsiveness to that will. An issue for congregational leaders is often to decide which labels are most useful in getting the congregation unstuck. Sometimes, as in the disease concept of alcoholism, the language of pathology can help remove shame and suggest the need for an outside cure. The language of sin and evil can be similarly helpful if it leads us to turn to God for deliverance from problems too big for us to handle alone. The language of stuckness helps us think systemically about the involvement of us all in both the problem and in any real solution.

The more stuck the system, and the more appropriate the labels "pathological" or "evil," the more denial and deceit play a part, and the more futile and dangerous are the use of direct, straightforward styles of leadership and reliance on ourselves alone. Straightforward approaches may be naïve. Careful listening and observation can guide us in deciding how subtle an approach to take. "Be wise as serpents and innocent as doves" (Matt.10:16b).

As a general rule, unless the situation is known to be systemically sick or evil, it is often simplest and most respectful to start with a straightforward, direct, and rational attempt to point out stuckness and to persuade partners in ministry to agree on a definition of the problem and a reasonable, common sense strategy.

Symptoms of Stuckness

Some common symptoms of stuckness in congregations today include the following:

- Conflict and scapegoating that recycle
- Absence of older youth and young adults from worship and other programs
- Inability to integrate new members of diverse backgrounds and to involve them in mission and ministry
- Declining membership, worship attendance, or giving
- General boredom at worship and lack of playful fellowship

- Cliquishness
- Lack of a clear and shared sense of vision, mission, and church self-definition
- An inability to include and minister effectively to a wide range of ages; temperaments; and racial, ethnic, and socioeconomic groups
- Preoccupation with maintaining buildings and raising funds
- Continual comparisons to the way things used to be and attempts to recapture the past
- Clinging to traditions and methods that no longer work
- Lack of interest in adult education, especially Christian living and theologically based process skills

Most of these symptoms do not by themselves prove that a congregation is systemically stuck. Each may simply point to a difficulty or challenge that must be faced. The fact that a congregation is declining in membership or struggling financially does not necessarily mean that it is stuck. But if several of these symptoms appear together, we as congregational leaders ought to wonder whether a systemic stuckness is creating the symptoms.

What Is a Stuck Congregation?

We can view stuckness in a congregation from many angles. First, we can see stuck congregations in terms of impasses in decision making. Peak of Life Church had a long history of division over leadership style and church priorities in the extended clan that made up its core membership. No vicious conflict was apparent, but the congregation could not decide what to do about its sanctuary, which needed repainting. Members were in a dilemma: The old-style decorations could not be retained, but neither could they be given up, because to do so would be to relinquish too much of the congregation's valued heritage. Although no one articulated this viewpoint, some felt that changing these decorations would betray long-time loyalties to departed members. The polarized congregation did nothing for years. The impasse was intertwined with the invisible loyalties and with either/or approaches to problem solving.

This deeper division showed itself when the decision-making processes for change got stuck. The congregation needed help to generate solutions because members assumed that some group would lose either way. This argument, with which it had coped successfully for years, did not by itself make the congregation stuck. If the pastor had sided emotionally with one group, the decision might have been made, but the congregation would have been polarized in win/lose thinking. When the pastor refused to take sides but held up the concerns of both sides fairly, a compromise was generated by informal discussion and adopted in a congregational meeting. Certain parts of the painted detail were preserved. Happily, a member who was a gifted artist volunteered to do the painting, and the congregation avoided turning a minor division into a major crisis.

Stuckness can also be viewed from the perspective of stages in the development of authentic community, as described by M. Scott Peck in *The Different Drum*. Peck suggests that for authentic community to develop, group members must be committed enough to one another to go through phases of pseudo-community, chaos, emptiness, and finally community.[1] A church may get stuck at any of the first three stages. Most, I suspect, get stuck at the first stage, pseudo-community. When stuck in chaos or emptiness, they often try to revert to pseudo-community, or they dissolve. Pseudo-community involves superficial or idealized relationships, and warm, fuzzy feelings untested by conflict or disappointment.

If we are unwilling to wrestle with each other as Jacob wrestled with the stranger at the Jabbok (Gen. 32:22-32), unwilling to let go until we receive a blessing, we will remain stuck in psuedo-community, unfinished conflict, or disillusionment. How many congregations have settled for pseudo-community?

A third way to describe stuckness is as the emotional constriction of a group in which people do not openly share relevant feelings and information and do not risk sharing creative ideas, lest they be squelched. God's love and creative energy do not flow with much freedom in such churches. "Negative" emotions like anger, fear, or pain may be denied, leading to group depression or demoralization, but so too may feelings like love and joy. Indeed, our capacity for love and joy rarely exceeds our capacity to feel the more difficult emotions. Those who have been forgiven much, have hurt much, and have found healing are those who can love and rejoice most deeply.

The degree of emotional freedom does not depend on the level of informality at worship. Formal structure in certain areas of congregational life may provide boundaries within which to feel emotionally free

or may allow emotional freedom in other areas to contribute to an overall balance. Congregations without much formal structure and with an
emphasis on spontaneity can become every bit as rigid in their informal
norms as highly structured congregations. Emotions can be covered up
just as well by noise as by silence. Emotional constriction can be as
severe when only positive emotions are allowed as when only negative
ones are. Emotionally constricted congregations do not simply need to
become more expressive. They need more honesty, variety, and wholeness in their emotional expression.

A fourth way to describe stuckness is in terms of ecclesiastical
narcissism—a congregation stuck on itself. Such a congregation is unable to move out to serve others in mission, and it is able to integrate
new members only when they can contribute to the congregation. These
kinds of congregations, like narcissistic individuals, have a distorted
self-love born of a lack of self-love. They suck the life and energies out
of members but are unable to make use of these gifts of love to heal and
fill their inner emptiness. These congregations' systemic processes do
not allow them to multiply and give back the love they receive. Narcissistic congregations are spiritual and emotional black holes. They are
stuck on themselves, and anyone who tries to fill this vacuum soon gets
pulled in. Such congregations need to develop selfhood, define who they
are, and learn to love themselves until the love overflows.

A fifth approach is to talk about addiction in organizations, as in
the writings of feminist and cultural critic Anne Wilson Schaef.[2] She
points out that both substances and processes can gain such control over
us that we feel we must be dishonest with ourselves or others about
them. Anything that serves as a "fix" to ease our pain and that distorts
our reality to do so can become addictive. Congregations can get stuck
because members or leaders are addicted to a substance and increasingly
draw others into the web of dishonesty and manipulation they weave to
cover up and sustain the addiction. Congregations that are naïve about
the power of addiction and unprepared to place boundaries on addicted
individuals can find themselves held emotionally hostage to the members' unrecognized addictions.

This is true whether the problem is sexual addiction, workaholism,
co-dependence, or addiction to negativity or self-righteousness. People
can become addicted to religion, prejudice, conflict, hate, or caretaking.
Pastors can become addicted to congregations, and congregations can

become addicted to a pastor or to denial, dishonesty, control, gossip, or emotional triangulation (i.e., managing anxiety through third persons inappropriately involved).

Viewing stuckness as forms of addiction implies that stuck congregations are powerless to overcome their problem and must rely on God's power in a process of continuing recovery. Of course, the need to depend on God's grace day by day fits the professed theology of most congregations and is often applied in the lives of individuals. Ironically, it has not often been applied to the systemic, corporate self of congregations. Individuals who are well along in a 12-step recovery process may be an excellent resource for congregations that wish to begin dealing with their organizational addictions.

A sixth perspective on stuck congregations is to describe them as developmentally stuck in their life cycle and maturing process. A stuck congregation is unable to move from one stage of organizational and systemic development to another as its maturity, context, and calling change. This stuckness is parallel to the stuckness of families unable to restructure their patterns of relating to meet the changing needs of members as they reach a new stage of the family life cycle, such as when children grow up and leave home. When a congregation's membership or neighborhood changes but it clings to processes that serve only its old-timers and insiders, it may be developmentally stuck. When a congregation moves from a small membership—a single-cell organism—to a large membership but retains its single-cell structure with a large group of peripheral members surrounding a core power group, it may be developmentally stuck. The congregation needs help to differentiate (split up and reorganize the new complexity) into a multicell organism that is well integrated into a whole at a new developmental level.

A variation on this perspective sees a congregation stuck in the renewal process as spiritually stagnant. Such a stuck congregation is unable by faith to grieve, forgive, let go, or even "die" that it may step out and be renewed by God with a new sense of identity and vision. An element of trustful letting go is involved in any healthy developmental process, whether for individuals or congregations. Viewing stuckness as a blockage of the renewal process is especially appropriate as a spiritual perspective for the body of Christ, the One who gave up his life that he might be raised by God to another level of life for the sake of the divine purpose. It takes a strong sense of identity (or desperation) for an individual to let go spiritually. Many congregations are in danger of losing boundaries, focus, memory, vision, self-definition, and coherence—the ingredients central to strong identity for groups or individuals. Stuckness in the renewal process may be a failure of faith, but it may also be a result of the weak and diffuse identity processes in which some congregations get stuck.

Some Working Definitions

Stuckness can also be defined as being caught up in a problem that does not get solved and that becomes more entrenched the more we try to solve it. "Problem" here refers to a knot, dilemma, impasse, or deadlock created and maintained by the mishandling of some "difficulty." A difficulty is an undesirable state of affairs that can be solved through some commonsense action for which no special problem-solving skills are necessary, or an undesirable but common life situation for which there exists no known solution and which—at least for the time being—must be lived with.[3]

In this perspective, stuckness is a problem resulting from repeatedly mishandling a difficulty in a continuing feedback loop (i.e., a process in which information received from an action influences future action). The worse it gets, the more we try the same faulty solution. The attempted solution amplifies the difficulty into a problem. In most cases, some or all of those involved have a sense of being trapped with no realistic way out. A stuck congregation, whether the whole membership feels it or not, creates problems by its approaches to problem solving.

Each of these perspectives can be useful. Church consultant William Easum, in his wonderful book *Sacred Cows Make Gourmet Burgers*, says the church is stuck in bureaucracy and the attempt to control.[4] Stevens and Collins, in *The Equipping Pastor*, say the church is stuck because church systems keep laity marginalized and prevent pastors from equipping the laity for the work of ministry. They say the church needs "organizational conversion" and a "gracious conspiracy of pastor and people to bring about the required systemic change."[5]

It is more important to see how our words function than to insist on a particular way of saying or doing things. For the purpose of this book, I will define stuckness as stuck feedback loops (i.e., information from our actions is fed back and shapes more of the same) that turn attempted solutions to difficulties into problems. This overarching framework will shed light on various "solutions" overlearned and misapplied to difficulties in our congregations.

The key catchphrases used in the Systemic Brief Therapy model of the Mental Research Institute of Palo Alto[6] to assess and address stuckness offer an elegant, simple, inclusive, and powerful way to look at systemic stuckness: "The (attempted) solution is the problem!" and "Do something different!"

Externalizing the Problem

This model, as I apply it, identifies the usual causes of stuckness in sincere and well-meaning but also sinful and bound individuals and systems. My intent is to shift from focusing on individuals and vague generalizations to looking at specific interactions and behaviors. The questions are not "Who is to blame?" and "How can we control or eliminate them?" but "What interactions and behaviors are getting us stuck?" and "What will bring about positive change?" This approach biases us to "externalize the problem" and to distill it into solvable form. If there are going to be solutions for our stuckness, we will have to get beyond blame and work together to discover solutions and get free.

A friend engaged in full-time interim ministry told me of a turning point in her work with a small rural congregation that seemed stuck. At a well-timed moment during a church council meeting she said, "Well, if nothing changes, nothing will change!" The leaders' jaws dropped in unison, their breath was momentarily suspended, and their eyes widened in sudden recognition. Then came the flow of energy and talk of solutions. It was as as if a dammed-up river had broken free. Movement out of stuckness had begun.

The point is to accomplish the goal, not to get stuck on being right or having to reach the goal the one correct way. Congregations can learn to discern that even words with a spiritual and loving sound may function systemically to produce scapegoating, avoidance of responsibility, denial, overresponsibility, overdependence, and feelings of helplessness. We need to notice how words and actions function at the systemic process level, not just what they say on the surface. We need to widen the range of our flexibility and the possibilities we perceive of how God can work. If a solution produces fruit of the Spirit and works for God's purposes, then we need to be open to it even if it does not fit our preconceived notions of what is spiritual and what is supposed to work.

The Larger Context

Congregations that get stuck do not do so in isolation. Members have friends and extended family who are not members. Members are often deeply involved in institutions or groups in the workplace. Congregations are part of local, regional, and national and global communities. They are usually part of a denominational structure and a historic denominational heritage. They are also part of a fast-changing society. All of these connections play a role in getting and keeping congregations stuck or unstuck. Most of the time we as leaders do not have direct ac-cess to changing these larger systems, but it is important to be aware of them. First, this awareness can help us be realistic, humble, and patient. It reminds us of the complexity we are up against when we seek change in a systemic process that is reinforced at other systemic levels. Second, it can help us understand why we and our efforts alone are not enough. We need God's help and the spiritual resources of our faith.

Cultural and Spiritual Contexts

It is sobering to note, for example, that many parts of society support systemic "rules" such as racism or works righteousness in our local contexts. Of the many factors in the larger systemic context of stuck churches, perhaps the most important factor today is change—pervasive, profound, rapid, and accelerating. Much of this change involves the foundation and structure of the world in which we live. The degree of potential threat associated with these changes is tremendous, causing many to become overstressed and overanxious.

Today's immense changes include the transcending and dissolving of many boundaries by the electronic media. Systems at every level are becoming more connected. Hierarchies are being replaced by webs of information and connection. Such changes, combined with new thinking in science and philosophy, spur people to see the world as more interrelated and pliable. This change has been referred to as a shift in our fundamental "paradigm" or model of what reality is and how the world works.

Paradigms and this paradigm shift affect how we get stuck and how we should approach problem solving in our churches to get unstuck. If we look at the overlearned solutions of the old paradigm and the problems they led to, we can begin to see what to avoid as we seek new solutions and a new paradigm in the church.

A paradigm, in the sense I use the term, is not just a theoretical model but a whole system of beliefs, attitudes, social arrangements, metaphors, and problem-solving strategies that might also be called a worldview.

The governing image of a paradigm is often pictured in its version of God. The old paradigm can perhaps be traced to a synthesis of two versions of God. The first is typified by Marduk, god of the Babylonians, who brought order out of evil chaos by use of violence. The second is typified by the Greek philosophical vision of god as a "perfect" being untouched by movement, conflict, change, or any direct involvement in the processes of this imperfect, material world. These gods represent the ideals of domination (total control of others and of nature) and impassivity (total control of self and undivided unity).

Behind both ideals lies the notion that chaos (read "change") is a problem or an enemy and that control (by violence or by reason) is the solution. The old paradigm, whether in its more rational or its more violent expression, is governed largely by the image and ideal of control.

To solve the problem of chaos and change in nature, to gain the ideal of control, and thus to push back or "bind" the soul's anxieties (about death and limitation, vulnerability to physical danger, uncertainty, and ultimate meaning or significance), the old paradigm evolved ways of making reality seem more predictable and controllable. Everything had a position in hierarchies of value and social order believed to be divinely fixed. Reality was seen as being made up of "things" or objects that could be separated from us and then categorized more finely so that we could "objectively" understand them. To "understand" meant to neutralize mystery or uncertainty so we could predict and control the world's behavior.

These strategies seemed to solve many human difficulties and, indeed, as happens with paradigms, few could imagine that any other arrangement could be sane or morally good. The old paradigm was not all bad, and we owe many benefits to its strengths. The problem was, and is still today, that this paradigm of control and domination has created more complex problems, such as alienation from our bodies and the earth, which it cannot solve. The effort to gain complete control tends only to make things worse. In many respects, the overlearned solutions of this old paradigm have become the problem.

The Church Context

In the church, the old paradigm tends to fix God and the Scriptures into static phenomena we can analyze, predict, manipulate, and control, and to turn us into beings that can similarly be controlled by religion. It pursues the absence of conflict at all costs so the church can mirror to others the gods of control and perfect peace. We need to learn to move out of this paradigm to get unstuck and to do effective mission in a new global context.

The old paradigm has many masks. What looks new, such as electronic fundamentalism, New Age religion, modeling the church after corporate America, or superficially using a few systems concepts, may simply involve a new look for the old paradigm. The key is to look beneath the words and to recognize the belief that solving our problems requires mainly control.

To become new-paradigm churches, our congregations need to replace control and competition for control with the image of cooperation. Domination should be replaced by mutual empowerment, and caretaking should give way to trustful, mutual caring. Concepts that serve cooperation, mutual empowerment, and trustful caring should be embraced:

- Reality as holistic, mysterious, and systemic rather than reducible and predictable.
- Experience as dynamic and contextual rather than static and "atomistic" (divided into smaller and smaller units).
- Knowledge as relational and personal rather than objective and rational.
- Logic as both "either/or" and "both/and."

- Relationships as organic and reciprocal (more like trees, webs, and circles than like pyramids, lines, and sharp-cornered figures).
- Truth more as co-authored and shared stories that free and give life than as fixed propositions and official stories to be believed and internalized as absolutes.

This new paradigm includes many parts of the old (such as analysis, hierarchies, and control) but puts them together in a new way with new goals, new rules, and new preferred solutions. It involves a leap to a "higher" perspective, in the sense of being logically more complex and inclusive; consequently some of its ideas and strategies seem incomprehensible or dangerous from within old-paradigm logic. The relationship between these two paradigms is, in both logic and spirit, like that between the "flat-earthers" and the "round-earthers" of Columbus' era. Today's new-paradigm heirs to the round-earthers often frighten the heirs to the flat-earthers who, when threatened, believe solutions lie in using power tactics to regain control. In the short run, and for many practical purposes, the earth seems flat, but in the larger picture its roundness comes into view. The call toward the new paradigm in the church is a call to see God's bigger picture.

The God of the Bible (as a Christian, I see this especially in Jesus) is the antithesis of both Marduk and the Unmoved Mover. This God of creative love relinquishes control of others and is completely involved in our pain and struggles. This God, paradoxically, empowers and initiates the New Creation by these means.

Caught Between Paradigms

At this point, many of us are caught between paradigms trying to make the transition. For lack of clarity and out of habit, we fall back into the old paradigm from time to time. We may get impatient with the slower processes of building cooperation or nurturing growth and try to force our will on others. Or we may be frustrated by the complexity of learning to value and use the diversity of human types and gifts. We may seek a way to make unique persons conform so that we can feel more in control. Sometimes we leaders fear that chaos will gain the upper hand in our church if we do not "pull rank" to suppress a divergent view. We want to have the new-paradigm spirit, but we aren't clear how authority and control fit with it, so we revert to old-paradigm spirit when we see that authority or control is needed.

We are caught in a spiritual tug-of-war. Many of us are just beginning to learn how to use power appropriately in this new paradigm, and we should be forgiven when we fall back. But keep the following point in mind: These are ultimately not compatible paradigms, and the conflict between them should not be underestimated. These two primary paradigms are not simply constructed out of a few loosely related ideas from which we can pick and choose. They are belief systems in which the parts fit together in a coherent whole.

However much we struggle between paradigms, one or the other "spirit" will define our identity. We cannot have it both ways. Either life's deeper problems are solved through forms of domination, or they are solved through forms of reconciliation and cooperation. I believe the unacknowledged bottom line beneath many of the conflicts in our churches today is the conflict between these two paradigms.

Having stated this conflict of paradigms with an "either/or" statement, I must back off and admit another ambiguity. Real life is rarely an all-or-none, either/or matter. Think of yourself here. How often do your views or your feelings fit completely into one of the boxes others may try to put you in? I do not wish to contribute to more of the double binds that grow out of simplistic thinking. I do not want to suggest the existence of two camps of people, one purely new paradigm and the other purely old paradigm. People's minds are messier, their edges fuzzier, and their behavior more confused than that. It is the paradigms, not the people, that are clear-cut and ultimately incompatible.

Let those of us who share this new-paradigm vision be realistic about the conflict between paradigms, be prepared with a patient vision of the difficulty of this struggle. Loren Mead, former head of the Alban Institute, says, "I believe that the turmoil around us is at least partly God's invitation to us to join in the New Creation."[7]

Let's join to help create a climate for new paradigm problem-solving in our churches and synagogues.

Questions

1. Is your congregation/church stuck? If it is, can you describe this stuckness in terms of the phrase "the solution is the problem"?

2. Can this stuckness be addressed openly and directly or does your core leadership need to develop more subtle and strategic ways to address it?

3. Is your congregation's leadership open to explore new "off-the-wall" ways to be faithful in mission? Brainstorm a few ideas that seem "crazy" at this point.

4. How is your congregation's emotional system responding to rapid change in society?

5. How are old-paradigm and new-paradigm visions coexisting in your congregation?

6. What would it take for your whole congregation/church to embrace a new-paradigm vision for problem-solving?

CHAPTER 3

Systems Thinking

The way we think about emotionally connected groups like families and congregations greatly affects whether we are able to cooperate, act creatively, and get things moving in a constructive direction. The dominant world view in Western society leads us to break reality into pieces, to focus on isolated individuals and on linear cause/effect explanations to gain understanding and control. Consequently, we have trouble seeing the larger picture and perceiving the interrelationships in the whole. This fragmented way of thinking blinds us to feedback loops, especially to the way we participate in and reinforce the very system we want to change.

For example, a pastor who expects mean-spirited resistance or mistreatment in the process of seeking change will probably get it. Whether by obvious or barely perceptible behaviors, he communicates this stance of opposing the congregation. His posture sets up a feedback loop of the type often referred to as a self-fulfilling prophecy. If unable to think about systems and himself as a member of a system, the pastor will probably look for a single culprit or cause and fail to see his own role in producing the opposite of the intended change.

Many approaches to family therapy can help us understand congregations as systems insofar as they are similar to families. I trained first in the approach called "Family Systems Theory" or simply "Bowen Theory" after its founder, Murray Bowen. It offers a clear and cohesive theory with seven interlocking concepts. Edwin Friedman, Peter Steinke, Ronald Richardson, and others have written excellent introductions to these ideas.[1] Many pastors have read these books. Bowen theory, as interpreted by these authors, helps us understand congregations as emotional organisms that often get caught up or stuck in patterns of *automatic* emotional reactivity. Bowen's concepts alert us to the power of anxiety to blur our thinking and our boundaries, and to our need to calm down and clarify both. He encourages us to break out of emotional triangles, the mini-systems we create to ease our anxiety by exploiting or excluding others and thus avoiding responsibility. He encourages us to keep in emotional contact with others but also to see the larger systems picture, to keep our thinking in control, and to lead by self-differentiation (i.e., defining who we are, owning and clearly communicating our thoughts, hopes, and feelings).

Understanding how "emotional triangles" work as a primary pseudo-solution to our anxieties, and knowing how to avoid getting emotionally hooked into them, can help us tremendously in finding true solutions. Emotional triangles stabilize an emotional system by distributing our anxiety in such a way that we do not have to take full responsibility for it or deal directly with those who raise our anxiety level. For example, once we have complained to someone else about the pastor, we feel we do not have to do the anxiety-laden work of talking with the pastor ourselves. Often it is helpful simply to remember how basic triangles are to human relationships (they are the smallest stable component of emotional systems) and how often hidden third persons and interlocking triangles are involved in our efforts at communication.

For example, when relationships in a congregation get stuck emotionally and communication breaks down, we need to ask what other emotionally involved individuals or groups are not being included or taken into consideration. If we do not deal with these third persons (some of whom may be from the past or from outside the congregation), or with our own roles as third persons in emotional triangles, our efforts to communicate and work through emotional issues one-to-one are unlikely to succeed. They will resemble attempts to persuade a couple to communicate when one partner is trying to find a "solution" to unmet emotional needs in a clandestine affair.

Bowen Theory is a valuable tool. But all theories have blind spots and lend themselves to certain tendencies of distortion. Bowen Theory relies heavily on the ability to "think systems" and to gain a high degree of emotional objectivity. Some who use Bowen Theory do so with warmth and humor (e.g., consider the storytelling style of Rabbi Edwin Friedman). However, some pastors misuse the theory to justify a stance of excessive emotional distancing, superrationality, and intellectual

superiority. The temptation to such misuse is particularly dangerous because these attitudes have characterized many of the solutions in Western cultures and religious groups (especially those of males and male-
dominated institutions) that have contributed greatly to widespread relational problems. I believe the MRI approach can help us place more
value on the spontaneous, playful, surprising ways that change often occurs and on the less rational-appearing and more counterintuitive, paradoxical solutions we often need. MRI Brief Therapy, the primary model
for my approach, traces its roots to the so-called Communications school
of family therapy that began at the Mental Research Institute of Palo
Alto, California, during the past 30 years.[2]

Focusing on Cooperation

Among the approaches begun at MRI, several visualize the family system as one that mainly resists change. They focus on so-called *negative*
feedback loops, which resist change by sending back messages that
discourage doing more of the new behavior.

The MRI Brief Model, in contrast, emphasizes systems' tendency
toward constructive change but also toward getting stuck in vicious
circles of so-called *positive* or escalating and reinforcing feedback. This
"reinforcing feedback" magnifies change within the vicious circle—that
is, it leads to more of the same—and keeps the system rigidly stuck in
that circle. For example, the more we fear grief feelings and suppress
them, the more we increasingly fear and suppress them, both as individuals and as a system. The MRI Brief Model focuses its interventions
on interrupting reinforcing feedback circles.

When we focus on the stuckness created by reinforcing feedback
loops, the bottom line is not the effort to fight and win a battle but the
desire to recognize and tap cooperation. The questions are: (1) How are
we seeking to cooperate? and (2) How can this cooperative intent be
used to achieve our shared goals?

General Systems Theory Concepts

It is beyond the scope of this book to provide a thorough introduction to systems thought. However, several concepts from General Systems Theory, developed primarily by the biologist Ludwig von Bertalanffy, can help us get unstuck and stay unstuck.

You do not need to understand all of these concepts completely. It is enough that you know that reductionistic, linear ways of viewing relationships often get us stuck, and that you begin seeing more systemic interrelationships. Wise and gifted individuals in every congregation understand these concepts intuitively, though they may use different words. These people can be tapped to help other leaders see the bigger systems picture. I doubt that it is possible for any of us always to think in terms of systems theory in this culture. It is a struggle for me even after working at it for years. I would caution, however, that if you are not growing in this type of thinking, you are more likely to misunderstand and misuse the techniques presented in this book.

The first important concept from General Systems Theory is that *everything is interrelated in a system and the whole has an identity that is more than the sum of its parts.* This concept has implications for congregations, such as that what happens in one part affects the whole and vice versa. It also suggests that congregations have a personality and a spirit and that members have a relationship with that spirit as well as with the parts of a congregation. Pastoral care includes not only caring for individuals and groups but also knowing and nurturing the spirit of the whole congregation. The congregation as a whole, besides individual members, influences how well a pastor leads. As one gifted pastor told me when I complimented his leadership, "This congregation loved me into being the pastor I am." He had a sense of the system's wholeness and what it meant for him. That sense contributed to his effectiveness.

The second crucial systems concept is that *cause and effect are not one-way linear steps in a chain reaction like one domino knocking over the next in a line. Cause and effect are reciprocal and circular. That is, they go both ways and move in a circle.* This concept has two main implications for stuck congregations. First, neither one-sided blame for problems nor one-sided credit for solutions fits the way reality works in systems. No person alone causes a congregation to get stuck or to get unstuck. We create stuckness or get unstuck together. Someone who dominates a committee or holds a congregation emotionally hostage can do so only because others do their part to allow or sustain the behavior. Leaders lead successfully only when people follow.

Sometimes the connections between events are so distant or subtle that we have to follow the circle back and look beneath the surface to see the connections. The remoteness of connection makes it easier to place blame on more obvious events or behaviors in closer proximity to the unpleasant result we notice. For example, we may blame the angry or depressed leader instead of noticing the part others play in this situation by subtly helping set the leader up to fail or to look bad by their passivity or secret gossip. Or we may blame a leader who announces a funding problem or confronts us with the need to face a conflict, instead of looking back to earlier leaders' failure to plan or to the congregation's implicit rule not to talk openly about conflict or ask directly for money. If we see how things fit together in a circular and reciprocal or mutual way and discern more of the larger picture, we will see that blaming distorts reality and does not help us escape a destructive circle. Blame may be a crucial part of the circular pattern in which we are stuck.

It is that circular pattern for which we need to look, rather than a single cause. If we begin to see this larger circle and the smaller circular feedback loops within it, we will see that any one of us in the circle can make a difference. We will see that we have many options for response because we can interrupt a destructive circle at many points. We will also see many points at which constructive feedback circles can be started. When we begin to understand the circular nature of causality, our creativity may be unleashed as we see many ways to approach the same outcome or to reach a goal.

Using Leverage

Because everything is interconnected in a system and because causation is circular, small change may lead to larger change, even to systemic change in the circular patterns that characterize the whole. This is the principle of leverage.

An illustration: As a boy I sometimes got the idea that I was pretty tough. A little neighborhood girl, several years younger than I, once demonstrated to me that bigger and stronger did not necessarily mean more powerful. She bet me a dollar that she could beat me up and make me cry "uncle." I looked down at her, laughed contemptuously, and told her the bet was on, thinking I would make a quick dollar. She promptly grabbed my left pinky finger and bent it back with all her strength. I cried "uncle" faster than you can wink both eyes and say "one dollar poorer." She had learned from fighting her older brothers to make the most of her small size and to leverage a small change into a large one. To her credit, she did not break my finger. She just wanted to teach me a lesson and gain some respect (as well as a dollar).

Although seeing the system as a whole can help us identify leverage points, attempting to change the whole system often creates a paradox that gets us stuck. We end up defeated, demoralized, and de-energized when we bite off more than we can chew. Knowing that small change can lead to systemic change gives hope to those who are realistic about our inability to handle whole systems. If the little girl had tried to fight me face on, as I expected, she probably would have gotten hurt wrestling in the dirt. For the swiftest, most painless, most powerful results, she needed to work at the point of greatest leverage. Even if one "lever" does not defeat the problem, small victories have a way of building confidence, morale, and momentum and leading to more small victories whose cumulative effect is large.

A group of rural churches devised a creative plan for a new cooperative relationship to help them afford to pay for full-time pastoral leadership and to strengthen their mission. The vision was inspiring at first, but leaders thought it could be digested whole by the congregations in a few large bites. The goals and timetables they set proved too ambitious. The plan hit passive resistance, and the leaders began to feel demoralized. Finally, leaders got together and asked themselves how they could zero in on a few meaningful smaller goals that could be successfully achieved.

They came up with a first step. They talked with a select group of patriarchs and matriarchs from each congregation who had not been in on previous planning, and asked each of them to host a fellowship meal at his or her home. Elected leaders and informal leaders were asked to attend, and time was planned for each host to talk about what the congregation had meant to him or her through the years. The meals were well received. Participants felt heard and began to bond. Throughout the small churches, members began to talk with enthusiasm about working together. Momentum began to build, and more steps were planned to continue building on it. The faulty solutions of trying to change too much too fast and of trying to bring systemic change from the top down (in a milieu resistant to such a style) were replaced by small steps from the grass roots up.

The MRI Brief Therapy framework—identifying patterns of attempted solutions that create or sustain problems and then reversing those patterns—is a highly efficient way of leveraging small change into larger, systemic change. When faulty solutions are interrupted by a new behavior, the rest of the feedback loop that they sustain is also broken up. Small strategic change often works to bring about larger change for another reason: These patterns of attempted solution are often embedded within numerous other parallel processes. They are duplicated at interconnected levels of a system. Therefore, change at such a point tends to resonate at several levels. In the case of these rural congregations, the changes the elected leadership made were duplicated by members who began to stop worrying about the huge change and started doing little things with people they knew from the other churches.

A smaller "stuckness" often is a metaphor for larger systemic patterns. In my training as a family therapist, one teacher would often use the homey example referred to as the "socks strategy." It consisted of focusing much time on the seemingly trivial task of getting parents to get their children to pick up their socks. By using this strategy, the family could move toward a change in structure so that the parents no longer felt bullied by their children but truly exercised leadership and supervision. This change in family structure led to constructive solutions to bigger problems in which the family was stuck.

If a congregation is stuck in one problem, such as scapegoating or conflict avoidance, it is more than likely stuck in the same sort of problem at other levels. Change at one level, then, if it is not too removed from the rest, may reverberate through other levels like the parallel rings moving out from a splash. We each carry within us, and tend to duplicate elsewhere, the spirit and emotional patterns of groups to which we feel deeply connected. If certain representative members can be enabled to work constructively through a conflict, even one that seems unrelated to the real issue, their efforts may snowball, leading to a positive effect on the larger issue.

At one congregation, Pastor James and Pastor Paul were caught up in a conflict between two factions—one more law-oriented, the other more grace-oriented. At a leadership retreat these two pastors came to understand that each had a valid point of view faithful to the Gospel and that their viewpoints complemented each other. Each began to tell people how much he appreciated the balancing views of the other. Gradually the factions began to follow suit, and the congregation's frigid emotional polarization thawed into a respectful disagreement and affirmation of differences.

Mechanisms of Stability

The third major idea from General Systems Theory is that *systems are governed by feedback mechanisms and processes (called homeostasis) that preserve their stability, balance, and sense of identity.* These mechanisms counteract change that threatens, or is perceived to threaten, the system's survival. An obvious illustration is the snuffing out of a new idea with those seven infamous words, "We've never done it that way before." Homeostasis, at the simplest level, works like the feedback loop in a furnace's thermostat. When the air reaches a temperature above the setting, "negative feedback" turns off the heat. Air that is cooler than the setting functions as "positive feedback" to turn the heat back on. Positive feedback amplifies or escalates behavior and emotion in a human system. Negative feedback decreases or de-escalates. These two kinds of feedback are used by the homeostatic force to keep the system in balance.

In human systems the feedback loops are powerful, complexly interconnected and emotionally "wired." Murray Bowen uses the image of interlocking human triangles that trigger one another to react in rapid succession or simultaneously, like electrical circuits. Human triangles, and interlocking circuits of triangles, are a special form of feedback loop. They are a way of handling the feedback of anxiety, and generally they work by excluding certain people from information and from the emotionally privileged "loop" to help others avoid facing their anxieties and to preserve homeostasis in the system.

Skilled family therapists regard with respect and even awe the power, ingenuity, and subtlety of the homeostatic forces in a family emotional system. Congregational emotional systems may at times be even more complex and elusive. Pastors or other church leaders who attempt to change a congregation's emotional system without learning to respect and use its homeostatic processes are likely to face much resistance to the change they seek. They may also get seriously hurt in the effort. A good rule: Never try to change a system until you respect it and understand how to side with its concerns while keeping your own agenda clear. Once people feel that their group identity is understood and respected, these balancing forces and those who play the key roles in them can work with you instead of against you.

A System Transformed

Systems, especially if they are open to information from outside the system, can also preserve balance and integrity by transforming themselves or by being transformed through the events that amplify the system's feedback loops (technically referred to as morphogenesis). This phenomenon gives hope to those dealing with stuck congregations. It means that if we can open up communication and feedback sufficiently in our congregation, the system itself might begin to learn. It might begin to transform itself, changing even the overlearned emotional rules that are keeping it stuck.

Even after what may seem to be chaos or disaster, a system may give birth to a new form for itself, better adapted to a changed environment. Crises and times of chaos may provide the necessary courage and opportunity to do something different. Devastating floods destroyed many buildings, including churches, in a prosperous city. Many old "walls" were torn down between people and churches, and new forms of cooperation emerged during efforts to save and rebuild the city. How often do failure, loss, and chaos provide fertile soil finally plowed sufficiently for God to seed new life?

As powerful as homeostasis is and as treacherous as efforts to bring change can be, there is hope. Open systems, like human systems, seem to have an internal "force" or "desire" for growth. It is as if God is pushing, pulling, prodding, weaving, and luring, from within as well as from outside the system. It is often a gentle voice, a flickering flame, but if we side with this force, the fire can grow to an intensity that the waters of homeostasis will not drown but keep in dynamic balance.

Systemic Levels

The final important concept from General Systems Theory we should know about is that of levels. *Systems involve levels of communication, development, organization, subsystems, logic, and change.* These levels are organized in hierarchies of complexity and inclusiveness. Higher levels both include the lower levels and transcend them. Each higher level operates by different rules of inner relationship than the lower levels it includes. Higher levels tend also to have more power by virtue of greater inclusiveness and complexity.

These various levels operate simultaneously within emotional and organizational systems. Levels can be aligned and confirm each other. They can also be misaligned and qualify each other, or they can contradict each other, making possible ambiguity and complexity of meaning in relationships and systems. In some ways, this ambiguity is rich and powerful. It increases our creative freedom and our capacity to express love, as in the various levels of meaning in poetry or romantic love. Ambiguity in relationships and communication also gives the receiver choices about how to interpret messages and behaviors. We can dull creative passion, decrease choices and responsibility, weaken our power to communicate and lead, and create paradoxes that rob us of humanity if we try to eliminate ambiguity.

At the same time, ambiguity allows us to send double messages, to make contradictory demands, to solve problems in ways that make them worse, and to pattern our relationships and organizations in ways that tie us in emotional knots and rob us of freedom and potential. Particularly pertinent to our discussion of stuckness is the fact that informal, indirect, ambiguous or hidden levels in systems often operate at a higher degree of complexity and trump the more formal levels at which we so often try to solve problems.

We can communicate on several levels (and on several channels at the same hierarchical level) simultaneously. We miscommunicate when we say one thing verbally but seem to contradict it with such nonverbal signals as tone of voice, body language, or timing. Every message in a relationship has both its literal content and an implicit message about the relationship. Literal content may be contradicted or modified by what is communicated at a nonverbal level. For example, a pastor may say, "God loves you, and you need not be afraid" verbally while saying with body language and voice tone, "I am angry at you and afraid, and you should be ashamed!"

Systemic rules in emotional systems also operate at implicit and explicit levels. At one level, there are rules for relating; at another level there are rules about who makes the rules and how. The existence of these levels creates the conditions for confusion and binds. One rule may specify, "We will say we believe in honest, open, and just relationships," while other rules say, "No anger will be allowed and no feelings will be heard from certain people," and yet another rule states, "We must not acknowledge or discuss these rules against feeling or expressing anger," and still another says implicitly, "Our small group with the money can change the rules whenever we choose, but no one may acknowledge this rule or challenge our right to do so."

Subsystem Level

Every system is made up of less complex and inclusive subsystems and is itself a subsystem of more complex and inclusive systems. Chinese boxes—each box slightly larger and enclosing each of the smaller ones —help us picture systemic levels. Of course, organic and human systems are made up of complexly interconnected systems, which do not always fit a simple sequential order and can be distorted if we try to force them into hierarchies of value. The Chinese boxes, however, help us think about the hierarchies of complexity and inclusiveness. The illustration also helps us picture the confusion, distortion, and exclusion that occur if we get the boxes out of sequence and try to make a smaller one contain the larger ones or if we jump from a small box to a much larger one. To picture how destructive paradoxes occur, imagine trying to make a small box contain a bigger one and the bigger one contain the smaller one at the same time.

Developmental stages in individuals, families, and organizations explain the idea of levels in a way that is closer to our human experience. Each new stage of development, to be healthy, needs both to include and to transcend the previous levels. There must be a discontinuous leap, a systemic change, so that the pieces are put together in a new way and function according to new rules of relationship. The old must "pass away," and something new must come into existence—for example, if the child is to become an adult or a small congregation is to become a larger multicelled organism.

In family therapy, developmental levels are often considered in connection to organizational levels of power, authority, privilege, and responsibility. It is easier to see in families how crossing up or misassigning levels can create problems—for example, when a child is expected to function as an adult or to act on the level of a leader or parent, or when an adult is relegated to the role of a child. Such confusion of levels results in contradictory messages, unrealistic and unfair expectations, and a host of other confusions and binds:

- The demand to leap over developmental stages to be accepted
- The obligation to be an adult and a child at the same time
- The expectation that one must be responsible for tasks which one lacks the power and ability to perform

Similar crossing up of levels can occur in congregations when individuals are asked to jump to a higher level of leadership without the opportunity to develop their skills through training and experience at lower levels with less responsibility. Levels of authority may be inverted when young people or inexperienced members are allowed to undermine official leaders and dictate group decisions simply because they make a fuss or form hidden emotional coalitions with other disgruntled members to help force their agenda. Sometimes members without official authority skip over the level of official leaders and use emotional manipulation to hook into a higher judicatory official so they can force their agenda on the authorities in the congregation.

Phillip was a dedicated administrator for his church's judicatory. Alarmed by a secret letter several members sent complaining of their pastor, he visited the congregation to try to help. Phillip catered to the complainants. The pastor was excluded from the ensuing discussions, and Phillip's very presence was used by the complainants to argue the validity of their complaints and their attempted solution. The pastor sensed that his credibility and authority were somehow being undermined by this process, but Phillip later blamed the pastor for the problem and credited himself with solving it. The pastor was disturbed by what went on but could not convincingly put into words what went wrong with the process.

The systemic problem was that the attempted solution involved an inappropriate "cross-level" coalition, with one level of authority skipped over and a higher level used to trump it. The higher administrator's anxiety was tapped to manipulate him. The process was also kept murky as attention centered on the content of the complaints, and discussion of the process itself was avoided. Clarity, consistency, and support among the hierarchies of power and authority at the official organizational level (and at unofficial levels) would have helped this situation—and can do much to free up other systemically stuck congregations.

The notion of systemic levels can help us see more options and devise a better solution. When we are stuck on a problem, we may need to ask what other levels are involved and approach the problem at a different systemic level, at several levels simultaneously, or with a strategy of a different logical level. For example, a pastor may think he or she has tried everything to bring about change in a congregation but may have only been approaching the congregation through the pulpit or the governing board. He or she may never have tried making the approach through key subsystems—the women's group, the youth group, the senior citizens' group, or the former congregational presidents. Or the pastor may have tried only direct approaches and no indirect or paradoxical ones that would allow communication on more than one level.

One pastor, when introduced to the concept of systemic levels, was able to see that he had been trying to produce a greater degree of teamwork by his own isolated efforts. Thus, he was sending contradictory messages on the levels of what he said and what he did. He immediately began asking other leaders to help plan how to achieve greater teamwork, and teamwork began to happen.

Contradictory Levels

Levels can simultaneously contradict each other, deny the contradiction, forbid recognition or mention of the resulting dilemma, or deny that such a rule exists. Thus is allowed the creation of "double binds" or paradoxes that trap and dehumanize us. We experience the disturbing stuckness of double binds ("damned if we do and damned if we don't") when contradictory messages are heard at different levels and we feel we cannot escape the contradictory demands or cannot comment on the contradiction.

First-Order and Second-Order Change

Perhaps the most important application of systemic levels for our purposes is the distinction between "first-order" and "second-order" change. First-order change does not change the system. It leaves the rules, patterns, templates, and overall character and spirit of the whole intact. First-order change may involve considerable change in terms of quality, speed, and variety at a superficial level without changing the system's major rules or patterns.

Second-order change alters the system itself, moving it to another logical level, or another level that includes but transcends the previous level. Second-order change alters the rules that govern relationships in the system—repeated patterns that serve as templates or emotional genetic codes for future relationships. It changes the whole whose character and spirit imprint the parts.

An example of first-order change: In a square dance people move in and out and around, each with a unique style, but the rules and basic patterns of the dance remain in place. Emotional games share these features. New players enter, and old ones leave. Players may trade positions, but the game with its rules, roles, and rituals stays the same. It is not difficult to see that congregational fights are often like games, with the players changing through the years as the ritual or the game continues with the same rules and roles and predictable outcomes.

People need rituals. Those involving only first-order change are not necessarily bad unless the system is locked into them in such a way that it is unable to make second-order change. If the system is unable to learn new solutions, if it does not value risk, experimentation, and novelty sufficiently to foster second-order change, if there is no higher level of rules (meta-rules) for changing the rules, it may get stuck trying to apply first-order solutions to a situation that requires second-order change.

The situation is analogous to that of a dreamer stuck in a nightmare, able to scream, run, and fight (first-order change) but unable to wake up (second-order change). Other analogies are the first-order change in car speed versus the second-order shift of gears; a religious conversion (second-order change) versus an accumulation of extensive information about God or religion (first-order change); a shift to living by God's grace (second-order change) instead of trying harder to "be a better Christian" (first-order change); a congregation's effort to get rid of a pastor (first-order change) versus changing the nature of its relationship with the pastor (second-order change). As these examples illustrate, each second-order change involves discontinuity, a leap from one level to another where a different set of rules and logic apply.

We often have a hard time conceiving of second-order change at all. Our difficulty lies in the fact that second-order change involves changing assumptions, leaving a given field of play and going outside the lines to find a solution. Second-order change is not just hitting the ball harder or running faster but playing by new rules or playing a different game. The classic example is the "nine-dot problem," which calls for connecting nine dots in a square with only four straight lines. The only solution is to extend the lines outside the assumed boundaries of the "box."

Even if we know about systems and levels, we will fall into impasses or paradoxical binds. Such binds occur when we try to apply second-order change to a first-order problem, as by revamping the organizational structure and by-laws of a congregation when the real problem is that the adequate structure and by-laws in place are simply not being used. We may also create impasses and binds when we apply a strategy that works for first-order change in an effort to bring about second-order change. For example:

- Trying to compel someone to love us by pushing or demanding it
- Trying to persuade someone to love and serve God from the heart by emphasizing God's demands and using fear or shame to motivate

Love and transformations of the heart require a leap to a higher level of logic and behavior.

These systems concepts are windows to a whole new way of thinking and seeing at all levels of life. I hope readers will work at seeing their congregations and relationships this way and help others grow in seeing this bigger picture. The chapters that follow assume this kind of thinking.

Questions

1. In what ways is your congregation more than the sum of its parts?

2. How might awareness of the circular nature of cause and effect free up your congregation to experiment with new ways of doing things?

3. What small changes might be used for leverage in your congregation?

4. Which people and processes keep your congregation on a steady keel? When have these homeostatic processes been less life-giving and more life-stealing? How can you honor these forces and still foster constructive change?

5. What signs of positive change do you see in your congregation? How can you focus on these changes and fan their sparks into flames? Does your congregation have rules for changing the formal and informal system? What are they?

6. Name some confusions of levels in your congregation or larger group. What might it mean for your leaders and your congregation to clear up the confusion and get these levels working together?

CHAPTER 4

How We Turn Difficulties into Problems

How do we get stuck? The answer on which we will focus in this chapter is that we get stuck when we mishandle small solvable problems or try to solve insolvable difficulties. Keep in mind the distinction between a *difficulty* (which we must accept and learn to live with, at least for the time being) and a *problem* in which we are stuck (created by mishandling a difficulty or smaller solvable problem). The self-reinforcing problems we create get worse the more we try to solve them. To find true solutions we must aim at changing our faulty attempts at a solution.

Sometimes in congregations, as well as in therapy, people seek help for difficulties that cannot be solved but must simply be lived with. If they keep treating these difficulties as problems to be solved, they will get stuck. They need help to see difficulties for what they are and to distinguish them from solvable problems. Here, for example, is a difficulty: When the pastor is not gifted as a preacher, small improvements may be made, but to some extent, members simply need to learn to live graciously with this shortcoming. A problem may develop if a cycle of criticism and feelings of rejection complicates the picture, leading to even more inept preaching and more criticism and feelings of rejection.

And here is a solvable problem: A member withdraws and refuses to communicate with the pastor, or criticizes the pastor to others about an unattractive personality trait. This action leads others to focus on the negative trait and creates discouragement in the pastor, magnifying the trait and creating a destructive feedback loop. The more the loop revolves, the bigger the problem becomes and the more stuck the relationship.

Understanding the distinction between difficulties and problems may itself break us out of the cycle of making things worse by the way we react. Distinguishing one from the other can help us step back and accept graciously what we cannot change. Such acceptance often leads unexpectedly to positive changes in the behavioral/emotional system.

Three founders of the Brief Therapy Center of the Mental Research Institute of Palo Alto (Paul Watzlawick, John Weakland, and Richard Fisch), in their masterful analysis *Change: Principles of Problem Formation and Problem Resolution*[1], have identified three basic ways that difficulties are mishandled and turned into problems:

- "Terrible Simplification": denying that a problem is a problem (turning mountains into molehills).
- "The Utopia Syndrome": trying to change a difficulty which, for all practical purposes, is either unchangeable or nonexistent (turning molehills into mountains).
- "Paradox": committing an error in logical typing (a technical term from formal logic). Action is taken at the wrong level in the system—for example, by failing to distinguish whether a problem should be addressed at the molehill, mountain, or mountain-range level, using tools appropriate to that level.

The notion of logical typing is drawn from the Theory of Logical Types, developed by philosophers Bertrand Russell and Alfred North Whitehead. The first type is a single term or, for work with human problems, the individual. The second type is a class of individuals—for our purposes, relationships. The third type is a class of classes, paralleling our use of the word *system*. In other words, each logical type includes the previous types but cannot be included by them without creating a logical paradox. For instance, a congregation's formal groups are included in its informal emotional system, which is included in the congregation, which is included in a larger judicatory (synod, presbytery, diocese), which is included in a denomination, which is included in the Christian religion, which is included among religions.

If we try to include all of religion or Christian religion under one of the previous types, such as a denomination or a congregation, we fall into the logical muddle or paradox that one denomination or congregation constitutes the whole of Christianity or religion. (Some religious groups seem to operate on such a theology and consequently become prone to paradox and dysfunction.) A more frequent problem of paradox arises when congregational leaders act as if the informal emotional system were contained in the formal boards and committees, which usually are, in fact, less complex and inclusive than the informal groupings.

In "Terrible Simplification," action is needed but is not taken. For
example, one pastor expresses great pain to church officers about the
behavior of a staff member, but the officers ignore the issue, thinking it
will go away, and the situation deteriorates. In the "Utopia Syndrome,"
action is taken when it should not be. A pastor tries to solve what she
sees as a lack of commitment by urging members to take immediate action when, in fact, the members are wisely going slow to make sure they
take the right action. In "Paradox," a first-order change, at the commonsense level of content, is attempted when the situation can be solved
only by change at a higher logical level. Or, alternatively, a second-
order change (which usually requires action contrary to common sense)
is attempted when first-order change would be appropriate. For example,
a church council may attempt to fix an ailing program by starting a new
program when all that was needed was to encourage and support the
present program leaders.

Double Binds on the Rise

Of these categories, the third is especially relevant. Many problems
faced in a time of radical change are problems of paradox. They stem
from trying to apply first-order change solutions favored by the old
paradigm to new kinds of difficulties that require second-order change
solutions.

First-order change is change in the content of relationships. Second-
order change is change in the structure of the relationship itself, how it
works. For example, a senior pastor may try to exert more control over
an associate pastor who does not meet his expectations. The associate
pastor's work deteriorates because she feels unsupported by the senior
pastor. This problem needs to be addressed at the level of second-order
change in the nature of the relationship so that it involves more respect,
feedback, encouragement, and support.

This point is especially crucial as we make the cultural transition to
a more cooperative paradigm between men and women. However, the
more the problem is addressed as a problem of control, the more disturbing the paradox becomes for both pastors, especially for the associate,
who feels that she must sacrifice a truly cooperative relationship (and
part of herself) to appear cooperative. The senior pastor feels that he is

being pressured by the associate to relinquish his proper authority and supervisory role in order to have his authority respected at all. Meanwhile, few of us have experience in solutions that counter or undo destructive paradoxes that arise from such situations.

When we attempt to deal with a difficulty by taking action at the wrong level, we often create pathological paradoxes or "double binds." In a true double bind two mutually exclusive demands are made, neither of which can be avoided. In addition, it is demanded that this dilemma not be named or discussed. Paradoxical binds are common because of the way people can experience several conflicting feelings at once. Conflicting messages can be conveyed simultaneously at different levels. These paradoxes move beyond being difficulties and become problems in which we are stuck when the situation's emotional rules prevent us from talking about them or even identifying what is happening. Great relief often results as soon as a bind is recognized and articulated, even if the dilemma persists. In cases where the rule against recognizing and articulating double binds seems inescapable, they may be extremely disturbing and even contribute to mental illness or behavioral disorders.

One lay leader felt he had to serve the agendas of both a group that wanted to get rid of the pastor and a group that was intensely loyal. Yet he felt he could not discuss the conflict openly, lest his congregation be shamed and he be blamed for its troubles. He also felt that mentioning anyone's name as he aired complaints to the pastor would violate confidentiality. Thus, direct action toward reconciliation was excluded. No one voiced these rules, but he felt they were firmly assumed and that he should not speak of them himself, lest they be denied. In the end, no one was pleased. The pastor left feeling hurt. The destructive conflict continued. The lay leader, suffering from burnout, wanted never to serve in such a role again.

What often happens to make such situations intractable is that double-binding paradoxical messages come from both sides of a relationship and interlock without our awareness. Frustration and double-binding communication from one side engenders similar reactions from the other side in a mutually reinforcing loop. These reciprocal or mirror-image double binds are possible largely because, besides the content of what is said, an implicit relationship-defining command is delivered at the process level of any spoken message in an emotional relationship. Mutual emotional commands are implicit in any ongoing relationship

of significance simply because we always try to structure the relationship to meet our own emotional needs.

We implicitly say, for example, "Take care of me," or "Accept me
as your caretaker." For good or ill, emotional health is affected to the
degree that our mutual, implicit commands fit or clash, and to the degree
that we are honest or dishonest, aware or unaware of these emotional
demands.

Pastors frequently get caught up in such binds or help to create
them for others. The relationship to the pastor is an emotionally charged
one for many members. It ties in with the unresolved and unnamed emotional needs and dependencies of both members and pastors. As families
and communities break up, the frequency and intensity of such unful-
filled and unrecognized needs rises, creating the potential for emotional
binds and unrealistic pressures on pastors to meet these needs.

Pastors and congregations are also prone to create such binds because of unspoken, religiously rationalized rules about anger, conflict,
grief, and sexuality which keep us from discussing our feelings openly.
Many pastors can look back at the apparent smiling niceness of a secretary or a member who, they know now, was angry underneath but
would not (or could not) admit it. The passive-aggressive behavior that
expressed this anger (often indirectly or by tasks left undone) was always followed by the implicit or explicit denial of any malign intent.
The pastor could not figure out what was going on, was unable to address the anger, and began to feel a bit crazy.

Double binds are created also by the complex and conflicting
expectations we have of church leaders. We may be unaware of these
expectations, or unwilling to admit them publicly. Unrealistic and conflicting expectations seem to be on the rise. A common example: Pastors
are getting the message that they must do more pastoral tasks well and
meet more of people's needs because so many are stressed out. Demands
for competence escalate while the rewards of the pastoral role—credibility, status, and power—decline, and the role itself becomes less clear. It is
increasingly difficult to know when a pastor has done enough. Some
clergy seek to address this situation by trying harder to learn more and
to do more so they can meet more needs. In the process, they burn out if
they feel sufficiently praised for their efforts and respond by increasing
their workload. They may also burn out if more effort produces fewer
results. Or they become embittered and depressed when their efforts go

unappreciated. Complaining about the situation may be regarded as un-
pastoral and sinful. Many pastors are in a no-win paradoxical bind.

What is needed is not simply to try harder or to learn more or even
to acquire more of the traditional pastoral skills. These would be first-
order changes. Rather, pastors need to jump to another level that lifts
them out of the dilemma. The leap requires that they do something entirely different, at another level of logic and communication. Doing
something different may mean doing less but doing it more strategically.
One pastor may need to admit stuckness and seek help. Another may
need to become playful and experimental instead of serious and cautious. Yet another may decide to ask members to pitch in and share the
load. More than one church has begun to come unstuck from overdependence on clergy when its pastor became ill or experienced a crisis
and admitted the need for help, and members learned to minister to and
with the pastor in new ways.

There is no one way to "do something different." Discerning a truly
different solution depends on first ferreting out what was tried and is not
working, and then ceasing or reversing those efforts. "Doing something
different" may require us to go against common sense, which is not easy
to do if we do not understand paradox in emotional systems. The skill
most needed in such dilemmas is the flexibility and creativity to make
the discontinuous leap to second-order change.

Terrible Simplification

"Terrible simplification" can be illustrated by one small-town congregation that called a new pastor. Many people came to love and admire
him, and the trust grew. After several years of what seemed a happy
relationship between pastor and people, the unthinkable happened. A
woman came forward and accused him of sexual harassment and misconduct with her. The group had no formal means of handling such an
accusation. It did have an informal method, however. The accusation
was denied. Furthermore, the woman who brought the accusation was
criticized, scapegoated, and driven from the congregation. This sort of
reaction had worked when members criticized pastors in the past, and it
seemed to serve well enough this time.

But the accused pastor eventually moved to a parish where the pattern of misconduct became more blatant. Hidden emotional and spiritual damage had been done to the victims of harassment and scapegoating. Members who knew and believed the initial accuser felt deeply wounded in their relationship with others in the church because of the way she was treated. These wounds and divisions had lingering and far-reaching effects. Many simply pulled out of the church. Not only did members lack adequate skills to handle such a crisis; they also did not know how to pursue reconciliation with hurting members who had left or become inactive. This mountain could have been moved if formal efforts had been made to listen seriously to the woman's concern while presuming the pastor to be innocent until proven guilty, and to apologize and make amends to hurt members later. But treating the mountain as a molehill prevented a healthy solution and created a bigger mountain.

Utopia Syndrome

The Utopia Syndrome is illustrated in many cases of congregational conflict. Congregations may develop systemic norms or unofficial "rules" that deny or suppress anger and conflict. Belief that we can achieve a utopian unity by our own efforts leads to attempted solutions that become problems. This happens in the biblical story of the Tower of Babel (Gen. 11:1-9), in which greatness and unity are sought through human effort. The builders believed they could raise a tower to the heavens and "make a name for ourselves lest we be scattered abroad upon the face of the whole earth." Their goal was so lofty and ambitious that God judged their arrogance. Ironically, the result of their effort to avoid being scattered was confusion of language and scattering.

The story of Pentecost shows the restoration of understanding and power as diverse people gathered humbly proclaiming God's praise. They focused on God's greatness and received unity as a gift of the Spirit. Each understood the praises of God, though different tongues were spoken; all were united and empowered in mission to go out into all the world with the Good News.

Rather than seek to solve disunity in a utopian manner or by our own efforts, the Gospel calls us to recognize the unity of the church as God-given, existing despite our conflicts and disunity. Our utopian efforts at problem-solving get us stuck in destructive paradoxes, disunity, and pseudo-community. Our prideful efforts to achieve and preserve unity often lead to destructive conflict and superficial versions of unity. Accepting the gift of community amid imperfection and conflict frees us.

Pastor Al accepted a call as associate pastor to Golgotha Church. After a few weeks, it became apparent that aspects of his personality and functioning at this early stage in his ministry triggered anxiety in Bill, the senior pastor. Pastor Bill tried at first to work out his anxiety by talking with the church secretary and a few others. But within a few months, he was using coercion in his efforts to bring Pastor Al under his control. The two pastors' theological differences and personality clashes could probably never have been entirely reconciled. But they were difficulties rather than problems at this early stage. The tensions could have been handled constructively. However, Pastor Bill's initial avoidance of confrontation, followed by his eventual attempts to control through domination, and combined with Pastor Al's angry resistance and refusal to comply, generated an escalating cycle, or vicious circle. They were stuck.

Pastor Al had been on the job only a few months. The two pastors barely knew each other. Al knew scarcely any members, and the conflict had extended to very few of them. This point would have been the easiest at which to intervene wisely.

Al's primary way of handling his hurt and anger was to resist control and to isolate himself to avoid embroiling the congregation. This reaction colluded with the system, allowing church leaders to characterize his hurt and anger as illegitimate and to avoid direct conflict. Even so, Pastor Bill and several other leaders feared that Al was dividing the congregation. In their panic, they escalated their attempts to quell him.

A series of power moves ensued as Pastor Bill and the president of the congregation tried to fix the situation. Al, becoming more fearful, angry and defensive, cut himself off further. This lack of communication heightened the other leaders' fears of a congregational division. They sought more measures to control the associate. The cycle escalated further.

The bishop eventually arrived on the scene, supposedly to mediate the conflict. When the pastors and the bishop finally met, the bishop told Pastor Al, "You have done nothing wrong, but we in the church do not know how to deal with conflict. So you will have to resign for the sake of the unity of the congregation."

The associate agreed and resigned in a demoralized state. After only four months, a few differences between two pastors had been turned into a serious problem. Unity appeared to be preserved by suppression of conflict and denial that the congregation was stuck.

As in most cases, this incident was embedded in a larger history and context. The congregation was still bloodied from an unresolved (and undiscussed) conflict involving pastors several years earlier. No wonder they feared the least bit of conflict and so readily accepted the systemic solution of scapegoating! Unfortunately, this "solution" prevented the associate from growing out of his tendency to withdraw and accept the role of scapegoat, prevented the senior pastor from facing his own anxiety about losing control and "image," and kept the congregation from owning its shadow side and learning more constructive ways to handle staff conflict. The beliefs that indirect communication was safer than direct and that the problem dissolved with the associate pastor's departure prevented a simple systemic learning experience, which might have led to change in this congregation.

In such a case, we can see all three types of mishandling of difficulties. Those that should have been dealt with seriously were denied until they got out of hand. Difficulties that could easily have been resolved or coped with were turned into large problems by fear and the utopian desire for perfect unity and a flawless image. Other minor problems were enlarged when solutions were attempted at the wrong levels—a level that treated human beings, relationships, and churches as things to be manipulated and controlled, and a level that entangled more people and higher levels of authority than necessary for a healthy and fair resolution.

The incident of Terrible Simplification described earlier in this chapter also led to a faulty solution of the Utopia Syndrome type and to various binding paradoxes. A young man I'll call Jake got extremely angry about what had happened at that congregation and left the church entirely for several years. Eventually he joined a congregation elsewhere. There he felt a powerful urge to dedicate himself to fixing what past experience had convinced him was wrong with the church in general. He built up credibility in his new congregation by hard work, dedication, and perfectionism in caring for the building.

All this time, though, he was suspicious of pastors and church bureaucracy. At some level he felt that the pastors were messing things up and that they needed to be scrutinized and held in check. The pastor of this congregation, Bob, was faithful and hardworking. He did not, however, share Jake's passionate concern about care of the building, and this lack of interest angered Jake. He began scrutinizing flaws in the pastor's performance, and he began to suspect a cover-up of something terrible that needed to be exposed. He feared greatly for the congregation's well-being.

Jake became increasingly critical of Pastor Bob and challenged him directly, demanding changes in how he did his work. Pastor Bob tried harder to please him, but nothing seemed to satisfy. Finally, Bob challenged Jake directly to cease his criticism and exaggeration. A power struggle ensued. As Pastor Bob became more upset and defensive, Jake saw further evidence to confirm his suspicions of the pastor's unkindness and anger. If there was one thing that Jake simply could not accept in a pastor, it was anger. Jake went "underground" to talk with others (to "triangle" them into his emotional feedback loop) and to elicit their own dissatisfactions with Pastor Bob. In this way Jake could temporarily channel his anxiety, reassuring himself that he was in the right as he tried to figure out what terrible problem was being covered up.

He sometimes drew out such complaints as:

"Things just don't feel right."
"I don't trust Pastor Bob."
"I don't like him."
"He was rude to me."
"He just doesn't seem like a pastor should be. I think he should have a different job."

Jake was unaware that his own anxieties and hints encouraged people to say such things. Nor did he realize that he took their comments out of context and shaped them to his agenda. He did not perceive that his reactions fed the anxious emotional atmosphere through an amplifying feedback loop he was instrumental in creating. The more he and others experienced this escalation of anxiety, the more they focused on Pastor Bob as the cause and the more anxious they became to do something to solve the "problem."

The young man and others with whom he spoke were near panic. Now the only possible solution was to circumvent Pastor Bob and "go to the top." Perhaps the council or someone "higher up" could make the pastor listen, expose the problem, and drive him out, if necessary, to save the congregation. The group took its concerns to the governing council in a surprise petition and to a denominational official in a secret letter. Group members called for a special emergency investigation.

With all good intentions but with much anxiety, the council and the official stepped in. By this time, Pastor Bob was feeling so hurt, misjudged, and wronged that he became angry and defensive at times and withdrew into depression at other times. His functioning as a pastor went downhill.

The council and the denominational official observed the pastor's behavior without awareness of how they were helping foster it, and began to conclude that he might indeed have a serious problem. A several-months-long investigation, undertaken on the basis of a petition from a small group, was badly skewed because of the manipulated conditions, and the pastor and council consequently suffered deep emotional wounds.

The investigation revealed a number of misunderstandings and personality clashes but no scandal, misconduct, or incompetence in central pastoral skills. In short, what had been only difficulties turned into a huge problem when a misguided solution was tried.

People were hurt. The church was hurt. Even Jake lost out. Jake believed he had accomplished something, and he most likely would continue this way of trying to solve problems in the future. Congregational officers tried to rationalize that they had handled the situation well, but no real healing was accomplished, and the resulting confusion and ill feelings lingered to the detriment of their growth and mission.

Jake was a highly anxious rescuer whose overlearned solution was to deal with anxiety by projecting it elsewhere and by making mountains out of molehills. He was aided in this debacle by the collusion of Pastor Bob, the local congregation, and a denominational structure. Naïvete on the part of church leaders about the manipulations of anxious and controlling individuals allowed the situation to get out of hand. They worked together to create an enormous problem as they mishandled difficulties. A large problem could have been avoided if the premature efforts to leap to the highest levels of authority had been blocked and attempts had first been made to deal with the difficulty at a lower level. At the least, sufficient information should have been gleaned to discern whether calling in a higher authority was an appropriate move.

Paradox

All three kinds of attempted solutions are often interconnected, carried out simultaneously or in rapid succession. One type leads to another or serves the other. The incident with Jake also contained, in its real-life counterpart, numerous examples of this third type of mishandling of difficulties. Pastor Bob was placed in several paradoxical binds by Jake and his friends and by his own assumptions, which led him to play into these binds.

One bind was the demand that Bob take charge and establish a "chain of command." In this situation, if Bob took charge he would, paradoxically, be allowing Jake to take charge by acquiescing and letting Jake's wishes define the nature of his leadership. What Jake wanted was leadership with less ambiguity, to quell his own anxiety and to increase his trust. Jake tried to solve his own problem of anxiety at the wrong level, since he attempted to change the wrong person (the pastor instead of himself). He also tried to accomplish a second-order change in the pastor (make him change his personality) by a first-order solution of increasing the forcefulness of his demands. Furthermore, no one was able or willing to articulate this impossible situation.

Pastor Bob, in various ways, also sent implicit, reciprocal double-binding messages such as, "You must like and validate me because I am trying so hard to please you." And later: "Trust me because I am commanding you as you commanded me to do." Bob's emotional neediness sent an implicit command that prevented people from spontaneously liking or trusting him. The harder he tried to be liked and trusted, the less likely others were to respond to the implicit command.

Such cases are often filled with crazy-making double binds, misguided attempts to solve a perceived problem. Hidden anger often plays a key role—as it did in this story, in which both sides became increasingly angry but tried to cover over their anger with niceness and rescuing. Both sides intended to solve the problem and believed expressing anger openly would be disastrous. Anger went underground and led to the delivery of indirect, disowned, and contradictory messages on the explicit verbal level and the implicit, nonverbal level. Complexity of communication, combined with anger disowned and denied, leads to many of the double binds we experience.

Type-three mishandlings can involve just the opposite, trying to impose a second-order or systemic change when all that is needed is first-order change. Such mishandling also played a major role in escalating the problem involving Jake and Bob. The complaining group had claimed that Pastor Bob and the congregation lacked an adequate formal system for getting things done. The council leaders appeared sincere in attempting to look at the situation systemically. However, before they really understood the failed attempts at solution, they began to impose various changes in organizational structure (second-order change). Unfortunately, this effort to force organizational change had been under way for some time and had not worked. A different approach would have been to back Pastor Bob and hold Jake and other members accountable to the structure and procedures already in place (first-order change).

A simple first-order solution, requiring the complainants to follow the established complaint procedure, could have effectively handled this smaller problem. Instead, it was turned into a major crisis. A congregation found itself stuck because a solution was attempted at a higher systemic level than necessary or appropriate.

Common Solution Attempts

It might be helpful at this point to list some of the most common attempted solutions that often turn difficulties into problems. Richard Fisch, John Weakland, and Lynn Segal of MRI have written a follow-up to *Change* called *Tactics of Change*, a how-to guide for clinicians that can help us here. *Tactics of Change* identifies five primary patterns of attempted solutions seen in the problems which therapists are most often called on to treat.[2] It also suggests examples of specific interventions that may be useful in each case.

Notice that, while there are some elements of types one and two, most of the patterns exemplify, at least to some degree, type-three mishandling and are best responded to with what might be called "paradoxical interventions." Here are the five attempted solutions they name:

- Attempting to force something that can occur only spontaneously (e.g. sleep, sexual performance, mood, or in the church, trying to demand that someone love God from the heart or enjoy worship).

- Attempting to master a feared event by postponing it (e.g., phobias, shyness, performance anxiety, or in the church, trying to solve anger or conflict by choosing not to deal with it).
- Attempting to reach accord through opposition (e.g., demanding respect or arguing to get agreement, as with a pastor's efforts to argue members into agreeing with doctrine).
- Attempting to attain compliance through volunteerism (e.g., "It's not enough that you do it—I want you to want to"; or waiting for volunteers to come forward without asking specifically for what is needed and inviting individuals personally to do a task).
- Confirming the accuser's suspicions by defending oneself (e.g., a pastor criticized for being unloving tries with hurt and anger, or even rationally, to explain why this is not the case. The more he denies the criticism, the more others are convinced of its truth).

In conducting brief therapy, I often run through this list and ask myself which of these patterns is at work, and we can do the same in the case of a church problem that seems stuck. We can ask:

- Are we trying to force a joyful and loving atmosphere or a free stewardship response rather than create an atmosphere that nourishes such spontaneous responses?
- Are we trying to deal with our pastor's alcohol abuse or a conflict of vision among members by avoiding the subject because it is too threatening or by passively waiting for him [them] to want to change?
- Are we trying to argue our people into unity or win support by defending ourselves?

Such questions can help us identify how we may be turning our difficulties into problems.

Good Intentions Aren't Enough

I suspect that one of the most common ways religious folk create problems is by misapplying labels like "sinful" and "bad" or attributing destructive intentions to those with whom they have an argument. Notice that people do not create the listed problems with a primary, consciously malicious intent, even if such an element may be part of the ambiguous mix. The commonly attempted solutions that become problems are based on sincere good intentions. Most of the time our misguided solutions are not evil. In all the examples in this chapter, people meant well and did what they thought was right. Yet leaders, members, and a congregation got stuck in destructive patterns. It is often most helpful to take pragmatic steps to correct these faulty solutions and avoid looking for blame or evil intentions.

It is helpful to know that most people mean well most of the time and do the best they can with what they have to work with, even when they bungle a situation. I use this point frequently in counseling, along with helping people put themselves in the other person's shoes. When illustrated with their own experience, this approach often helps people begin to understand, forgive, and get unstuck. It can be far more helpful than demonizing those who have wronged them. In therapy as well as pastoral work, I often reframe unhealthy rules and behaviors that people think are "loving" as "falling short of real love," or I use their intent to do the right thing as a lever to persuade them to adopt healthier, more loving behavior.

In a congregation, too, we can urge people to examine behavior that might arise from loving intents that became twisted. For example, members who criticize the pastor's sermons to others might be invited to show their "love for the congregation" and their "concern for good preaching and the pastor's continuing growth" by joining a sermon feedback group and sharing their views in a constructive way.

What about Sin and Evil?

I cannot end this chapter without noting one last crucial way congregations create problems by mishandling difficulties: They fail to turn to God to solve the issues of sin and evil. If most problems are created by mistaken but well-meaning people, does this mean sin is not involved and that we as leaders should leave the issue of sin out of the picture? By no means! The sins involved in such problems should be confronted gently with a call to repentance. But if we are going to confront sin, we should first learn to understand it from a systemic perspective.

I am not assuming a single definition of sin or evil. There are several meanings of these terms in Scripture, and each has its place. It is important to keep in mind that sin and evil are located not only in individuals but also in groups. These terms are most useful in getting us unstuck when they help us turn to God for help at the right times rather than trying to solve every problem by our own reason. On our own, we can improve communication and learn better problem-solving techniques. But when, underneath the stuckness, we find lies, willful unbelief, greed, sexual immorality, false teaching, nurtured bitterness, intentional revenge-seeking, individual and systemic addiction, pursuit of domination, and control-oriented coping—when such is the case, we cannot solve these problems without the resources of our faith traditions and God's power.

To see sin systemically, we must shift our focus from isolated individuals to individuals in systemic contexts; to the way broken relationships tend to involve both or all parties in the relationship. We need to focus on the way sin is expressed in the system's rules, the subtle collusions of going-along-with, the sins of passivity or omission; and the way sinfulness (such as self-righteousness or exclusivity) is expressed in the meaning, stories, and spirit of groups. If we do not conceptualize sin and evil systemically, our very use of the label will tend to become evil itself as we scapegoat others.

To think about sin and evil systemically, we need also to shift our focus away from seemingly obvious and intentional sins toward sins hidden behind or inside good and "loving" intentions. Sins like misguided and selfish love, self-righteous rescuing, anxious caretaking, protectiveness, passive-aggressive kindness, fear-driven refusal to risk, silent collusion, lack of active validation of others, shame-oriented or pride-oriented group spirit—these have often been neglected in the church's history. Such "soft" sins come into focus as we see how they function systemically to preserve oppression.

If we can understand these "masks" of sin and the ambiguous mix of motives involved in our solution-seeking behavior, we will be in a better position to understand how, as 2 Cor. 11:14 (paraphrased here) puts it, Satan disguises himself as an angel of light, convincing us of the goodness and rightness of our faulty solutions.

When Are Solutions Evil?

Sometimes what we believe to be a solution is sinful. This is so when we benefit at others' expense, when the "solution" solves some problem for us but creates pain or injustice for someone else (or for us later). For example, the totally homogeneous church may feel good to participants while blunting their awareness of the injustice and pain suffered by outsiders. Another example is the attempt to keep peace by denying the anger that belongs to one relationship and taking it out on an individual or group that cannot fight back. When we willfully persist in these sinful solutions and increasingly become bound to their destructiveness, they may take on complex systemic form and a change-resistant power for which evil is the only appropriate name.

We may be oblivious at the early stages to the fact that our solution is causing problems elsewhere. However, as we apply more of the solution and its problematic side becomes harder to deny, a progression toward greater evil may develop.

Some sixteenth-century church reformers used a three-part formula to describe the progression of evil. First it blinds. Then it binds. Then it destroys. The example of this threefold movement in the process of addiction is instructive since the substance or process being "abused" seems to solve problems, and people become blinded to the problems it creates farther down the road. Caught in the disease of denial or blindness, the person or organization becomes increasingly entrapped and bound chemically, psychologically, socially, and spiritually, even destroying the self and others to solve problems with a solution of choice. Much of the blindness and entrapment results from the social network in which the addict or addictive organization is increasingly intertwined. This network reinforces a version of reality that lends itself to addiction in the first place and makes it increasingly complicated for the addict to leave that lifestyle.

However, it is not only in the recognized addictions (to drugs, sex, gambling) that we see this progression into the web of evil. The same downward spiral is at work in sins of self-righteousness, prejudice, and racism.

Theologian Ted Peters, in *Sin: Radical Evil in Soul and Society*, traces this progressive nature of evil from anxiety (the fear of loss) to unfaith (when trusting becomes difficult) to pride (making myself number

one) to concupiscence (lusting after what others have) to self-justifica-
tion (looking good while scapegoating others) to cruelty (enjoying my
neighbor's suffering) to blasphemy (sataric rituals and the destruction
of the inner soul.)[3]

At each of these stages people attempt to solve some difficulty or
an aspect of their own sin. In emotional systems we can see how the first
stage, anxiety, is often mishandled and turned into a problem. Bowen
Family Systems Theory traces the course of mishandled anxiety in emotional systems. Unable or unwilling to face our own anxieties, we hook
others in and use them to ease our anxiety. We feel closer to them and
more justified in our actions as we collude to reinforce each other's
viewpoint and exclude or criticize someone who forms the third corner
of what Bowen calls the "emotional triangle." If the same people are
continually excluded or blamed and our own limited viewpoint is continually reinforced, then our solution may become their problem now
and our problem later. They experience the emotional injustice of exclusion and scapegoating. Our narrowness and prejudice are reinforced,
and we become less able to respect differences and more self-righteous
about our own views and behavior.

One obvious example of this stage in the progression toward evil
occurs in a church surrounded by American Indian reservations, or in
the midst of another minority group. The church strengthens its own
sense of unity and righteousness (finds a "solution" to its anxiety about
racial tensions and potential internal divisions) by avoiding outreach or
dialogue with these neighbors and by telling racist jokes when no outsiders are present. Such a congregation is stuck. Members feel less anxiety about their sins of oppression and more unity among themselves
vis-a-vis the outside group. In this process, the congregation gets stuck
in a progression of evil as Peters describes.

Another example: Shelly became hurt and angry because of gossip
she heard about a comment the pastor supposedly made about her. Since
she found it too threatening to ask the pastor directly what he had said
and meant, Shelly handled her pain and anxiety by talking to other
people who might agree with her and uncritically support her anger at
the pastor. This solution focused her attention, and that of the others, on
seeing an increasing number of qualities in the pastor about which to be
offended. The more she and they saw, the more angry and anxious they
became. The result was an escalating feedback loop. They were stuck

emotionally. They were also caught up in a progression toward evil which led toward increasingly self-righteous blindness to their own sins and to more scapegoating of the pastor.

The seriousness of a conflict and the likelihood that outside intervention will be needed is strongly correlated with the number of people who have been triangled into the conflict. If many people have taken sides emotionally, gotten emotionally hooked, and lost the ability to see from more than one point of view, the problem can grow to immense proportions and the people will likely become stuck.

At some point the triangling, the gossip, the "buzz," as one member described it, take on a life of their own like a swarm of bees one can hear but not see. The "buzz" can be perceived by some people as the problem, or it can turn a difficulty into a full-fledged problem. Not only do individuals become increasingly hardened in their positions by all the buzz; the tangle of triangles begins to congeal into a communal entity which itself may display signs of evil.

One person's solution to anxiety about a difficulty becomes another person's solution and then another's and, eventually, the whole congregation's solution and problem. In the example above, the progress toward evil in the congregation was short-circuited when intervention led to an awareness by most of those involved that the solution lay in hearing points of view different from their own insulated version, in members communicating directly with the pastor, and in the pastor's making himself more accessible and open to hearing difficult feelings.

Higher Solution Needed

Evil progresses not only internally but as people and groups are increasingly drawn into social networks and systems that hold to evil beliefs and practices. As people become involved with hate groups like Nazis or Skinheads or gangs whose official solutions involve racism and violence, the spirit of the group increasingly envelops and shapes that person.

Congregations are by no means immune from the progression toward evil as they repeat their favored solutions. An overlearned solution such as control or conflict avoidance can be used in increasingly evil ways. If we try to solve the problem of evil with psychological techniques or only at the individual level, we will add to the problem.

The innovative solution in many cases is to acknowledge that we as individuals, and sometimes even as a congregation, are powerless to solve our own problems and to call on the spiritual power of the broader religious community and to pray together for openness to God's spirit to guide, empower, and break the hold of evil. If we fail to seek solutions to evil at the social and spiritual level or try to solve them by ourselves, we have chosen the wrong logical level and inadequate tools. The various social levels and the spiritual level are higher, more complex, and more inclusive than the psychological level. Attempts that do not involve seeking God's guidance will not only fail to deliver us from evil; they will create paradoxical binds that bind us ever tighter.

Questions

1. Give examples of creating problems by trying to ignore or deny them; by trying to solve an insolvable difficulty instead of learning to cope with it creatively and graciously; by trying to solve a problem with a strategy at the wrong logical or systemic level.

2. Why are good intentions and hard work not enough to solve stuckness?

3. How can talk about sin and evil perpetuate stuckness in a congregation?

4. How might a more systemic understanding of sin and evil help us get unstuck?

5. Give examples of how sin is sometimes hidden under apparently good and loving intentions (e.g., to rescue or help others).

6. Is your congregation involved in solving some members' spiritual problems in ways that make them more arrogant or self-satisfied and indifferent to prejudices or injustices others feel?

7. How is your congregation relying on the higher power of God to solve its own problems of emotional/systemic stuckness?

CHAPTER 5

Paradox That Binds,
Pardox That Frees

Congregational leaders, and pastors in particular, are caught up in a societal and church climate that fosters destructive paradoxical binds. I devote an entire chapter to the type of mishandling called "paradox" because it plays such a key role in stubbornly stuck situations and be- cause rapid social change creates a climate that renders disturbing para- doxes increasingly common.

Naming the binds often helps free us even if the binds are not total- ly solvable. Pastors and other congregational leaders are often caught in binding paradoxes caused by general confusion about roles, limits, choices, and expectations. Among these paradoxes:

- Pastors are called to minister to more situations of acute brokenness than ever, although hurting people may resist participation and com- mitment in the church community that constitutes the pastor's greatest resource for their healing. Many congregations are so averse to conflict that they are unwilling to struggle to achieve a genuine community that could minister to broken people.
- Pastors need to master additional skills and lead more effectively, precisely at a time when the old-paradigm vision of authority is disappearing. Moreover, little clarity or support exists for defining the role of authorized and empowered shared leadership in the new paradigm. The bind is an old one: The pastor has responsibility for a task but is not given the authority to get it done.
- Pastors and congregations are expected by some to provide in- creased services and options at a time when less money is available. Moreover, they may be expected to raise the needed funds without asking too directly or too often.

- Churches and their pastors often feel pressure to alleviate people's anxieties and uncertainties by giving them solutions and absolute truths (à la the old paradigm) at a time when scholarly integrity requires us to recognize the ambiguities and complexities of language, Scripture, and tradition.
- Pastors and leaders entrusted to tell the truth may feel they must "be nice" at all times, pleasing the "customer" even if doing so requires a false front. They must never express anger, and they are to foster "unity" by avoiding conflict. If they fail in this effort, they risk being labeled hypocrites.

We are most free to deepen and enjoy our humanity when we can name and accept life's paradoxes (for instance, we are limited beings with limitless dreams; we can love and hate the same person). It is often our inability to accept and live richly with paradox that leads us to create binding paradoxes. The confusing transition from old to new paradigm makes such binds more common. According to the old paradigm, we should "solve" life's unavoidable paradoxes—uncertainty, unpredictability, ambiguity, complexity, pain, vulnerability, aloneness, helplessness, longings of the soul, and death. These cannot, however, be "solved"—they can only be lived with in more-or-less humanizing ways. People who live in the old paradigm tend to use linear, logical, fixated, analytic solutions, attempting to dissolve paradoxes to banish difficulties and to solve complex new problems that require paradoxical responses. Much misguided problem solving of this type occurs in the church and sets up a climate that creates double binds.

Four Square Church uses the Bible as a recipe book to tell people exactly how they should live. This approach reduces anxiety associated with ambiguous life situations such as issues of sexual identity. But several members' children who are gay or lesbian are thrown into the double bind either to deny their orientation or to be regarded as leading a shameful lifestyle. In either case, they are expected not to discuss the bind openly. Another congregation deals with difficult feelings associated with uncertainty and change by insisting that its pastor and organizational structure be in control. As a result, little occurs that is spontaneous, fun, and inspiring. Some members feel squelched, and the church remains stuck in the past.

Unavoidable and "Good" Paradoxes

We need help to live with unavoidable paradoxes graciously, coura-
geously, creatively, compassionately, and with humor. When we try to
solve them, we set up paradoxical binds that get us stuck. Leaving a
climate that fosters destructive paradox requires that we (1) live responsibly with limits and choices, accepting the unavoidable paradoxes of
being human, and (2) challenge people to recognize and take responsibility for their choices. People who deny limits and choices will foster
paradoxical binds.

The MRI Brief Therapy Model helps us recognize paradox as char-
acteristic of life and relationships and as playing a central role in the
solution of many stubborn problems. Those who use the Brief Therapy
Model often follow a paradoxical logic in their explanations and strategies, opening up new choices for problem solving. This method works in
situations where common sense approaches will not work. For example,
common sense often tells us to try harder and do more, or poses either/or
alternatives. Practitioners of brief family therapy know that trying harder or going faster often makes things worse, that we often must do the
opposite to get unstuck, that less is often more in therapeutic work, that
people often have excluded options that sound crazy or impossible, and
that dilemmas resolve themselves into mere difficulties when viewed
from a broader systemic perspective that shows them as both/and rather
than either/or situations.

Creating Binds

Those using the logic or common sense of the old paradigm tend to be
uncomfortable with paradox because it seems to leave life fuzzy and
uncontrolled. This logic sets up reality in terms of "either/or" and "all
or none" categories to eliminate ambiguities and engender a feeling of
control. Those who use this paradigm are particularly uncomfortable
with such paradoxes as "less is more." They reason that "more is more."
Their goal is to have it all. The old paradigm breaks reality into parts,
but only for the sake of gaining more control.

Totalistic Thinking

The old paradigm biases us to perceive reality and attempt solutions in ways that are technically referred to as "totalistic." By "totalistic" I mean thinking that encourages a belief that the whole is contained in one part, or that a situation must be perfect, complete, true, and absolute if it is to be valid. This "all or none" thinking can take several forms. We might believe we can sum up a person or group in terms of one trait, or consider one part of a relationship as the whole, saying, for example, "She's a pastor. I know all about these women pastors." Or: "He got angry at me. He is an evil person." We might insist on complete maturity or more independence than is developmentally appropriate for a person or organization.

For example, we might expect a child or a new worker or a young pastor or a mission congregation to accomplish a task requiring a higher level of sophistication without guidance, supervision, or support. We might also believe that we can have sufficient influence on others to prescribe or control their choices—insisting, for example, that people exhibit not only godly behavior but also appropriate expressions of contrition or love. We might believe that reality and relationships can be understood in either/or terms that exclude every other possible reality—for example, that pastors and fellow believers are either totally good, or they are totally bad and should be ousted.

Human life cannot flourish under such categories. Unless we accept that both/and paradoxes and limits or "partialities" are central to life and to the human condition, we will create destructive paradoxes.

When we operate out of the old paradigm and try to banish the ambiguities, limitations, and paradoxes that make us human, we create destructive paradoxes that confuse our relationships and prevent our best selves from emerging. When stuck in the old paradigm, we have trouble affirming that people are both predictable and unpredictable, beautiful and ugly, sane and insane, loving and hateful, saints and sinners. Since such paradoxes make life seem uncertain and uncontrollable and stir up a good deal of anxiety, we exclude them. We divide people into either/or categories and make demands in those terms.

What Bowen Family Systems Theory calls "triangulation" often exemplifies such thinking. For example, people in an emotional triangle assume, "Either you're for us or against us in our position about the pastor. You can't be on both sides." Those who avoid either/or beliefs can see reality in its ambiguity, and find it easier to stay out of triangles. This new-paradigm skill cannot realistically be expected of those stuck in old-paradigm logic.

Nor do those so stuck stop with one either/or demand when they are anxious or power-hungry. Totalistic ideas and expectations tend to pile up. For example:

"Either you are an all-loving pastor or an evil, uncaring one that we must get rid of."

"Either you are totally committed to the church, or you are no Christian at all."

"Either you are totally sane, or you are crazy. There are no degrees of mental health."

"Either you are a heterosexual male or you are a heterosexual female. There are no other options."

"Either you are nice and never angry, or you are angry and a bad person."

The either/or beliefs and expectations are often assumed but not articulated. Those who hold them may deny, when pressed, that they do so. Consequently, leaders may feel either/or pressures and yet not know the source of the feelings of stress. The inability or refusal of people to name these either/or assumptions, and people's tendency to blame the one who complains, render the assumptions even more crazy-making. Congregational leaders have their hands full to flush out such denied but emotionally forceful assumptions.

Double Binds

Degrees of bind depend on how and where either/or assumptions come together. For this kind of demanding, simplistic thinking to create what is technically defined as a double bind, several factors must be in place. First, the absolute demands must come within important, inescapable emotional relationships. Casual and detached relationships may display some of these characteristics and contradictions, but they do not create true double binds because they are not taken so seriously. Second, the recipient of conflicting absolute demands accepts them, at least unconsciously, as valid and binding. Third, the situation includes a rule that one absolutely must not name the bind (often at the risk of losing the relationship or the approval on which one is dependent).

The fact that we cannot name a bind or have its reality validated by others is the final "lock" that traps us. Totalisms tend to extinguish themselves like a fire running out of fuel when the assumptions are named, if they are not fueled with similar thinking from others in the environment. If these extreme beliefs and expectations on the part of the pastor or a few members are named openly and become a source of shared humor or conversation with members who can accept imperfection and ambiguity, the situation will probably remain tolerable.

If articulated, these totalistic expectations would often include the words "never," "always," "every," and "must":

"We want you always to be available in your office and also to be out with the people where you are needed."

"You must never complain or express anger about this situation. It is part of being a pastor."

"We want to put you on a pedestal, but we want you to be one of us."

"Take care of yourself and your family, but show that you put the congregation first or we will consider you unloving."

Once such expectations and the binding paradoxes they create are named, they are less able to disturb and draw out our worst selves. Once named, they can be tamed by open negotiation.

Prejudice, Collusion, and Reciprocal Binds

One of the most common types of totalism, one usually denied, is commonly defined as prejudice: overgeneralization from one or a few instances. The diabolical nature of prejudice can be more clearly seen when we observe its creation of double binds that bring out the worst in others and become self-fulfilling prophecies.

There is rarely room for innocence or self-righteousness amid the ambiguities of double-binding paradoxes. We collude in most cases with our own stuckness. Emotional binds are most powerful when we accept others' either/or assumptions. When the totalistic expectations and logic of others meet our own either/or emotional expectations and reasoning about ourselves, and the relationship does not allow us to name the conflict, a double bind is set and we are emotionally hooked. In many cases, a pastor will not only be bound by the conflicting demands of others but will also put conflicting and unrealistic demands on members. These reciprocal binds feed on each other in escalating feedback loops, where we become stuck.

Either/or expectations often are not articulated in emotional relationships, but when people are emotionally "needy," others tend to feel a totalistic demand in their expectations, regardless of what is said explicitly. For this reason, pastors and other leaders must take care to meet their own emotional needs, negotiating clear agreements, limits, and boundaries. If pastors set aside time for care of emotions with friends, counselors, and spiritual disciplines, they can better avoid getting hooked into the binds of trying to meet unrealistic expectations.

Totalism is closely akin to legalism, absolutism, and perfectionism. Preventing or freeing up double binds involves grace, humility, and humor. The individual's escape from the jaws of such dilemmas ("acceptance of limits," "letting go of needs") requires surrender, repentance, and faith. The appropriateness of religious language to discuss psychological binds is no coincidence.

Theology and psychology, when they rightly perceive life's complexity, look at the same fabric of experiences from different perspectives. When pastors learn to enjoy stories and laugh with their people even at their own stuckness, they have come a long way toward getting unstuck. When leaders admit they are really stuck and can't solve a problem, when pastors acknowledge they can do only so much and ask for members' forgiveness, when members recognize and revel in their leader's shortcomings, knowing these are signs of a common humanity, they go far toward staying out of double binds.

A Climate for Totalism

Double binds would be challenge enough for any leader. What complicates the situation today is rapid change and the current paradigm shift.

Many new totalisms become common in society as traditional roles and expectations break down and people become accustomed to high-powered entertainment and new ways to have their needs addressed. People disagree about what leaders can be expected to do for us and whether to judge them in terms of old-paradigm or new-paradigm values.

This lack of clarity about leadership and its limits wreaks havoc among clergy and in our churches. Worse, many paradoxical binds and impasses are created as congregations attempt to use old-paradigm strategies to handle difficulties arising from complexity and the new paradigm. Old-paradigm solutions often create problems because new-paradigm realities are of a higher level of complexity. Solving these more complex problems using old-paradigm methods is like using an auto mechanic's tools to solve the problems of a human body or mind.

Increasingly, pastors and professional staff are working with new-paradigm ideas, either because they have studied these concepts or because they are members of Generation X. New-paradigm folk expect to work, with "bosses" as well as with peers, under the new-paradigm model of partnership, mutual respect, reciprocity, frequent feedback (especially affirmation), cooperative teamwork in which everyone's gifts are used, involvement and belief in the mission, and mutual empowerment.

At the same time, many lay leaders and pastors still operate (especially in times of stress and crisis) out of an old-paradigm model of hierarchical leadership. Misunderstandings and reactions between people who assume different paradigms often push each side to extremes. One's perceived disrespect becomes the trigger for behavior by the other that is interpreted as disrespect by the first. Reactions escalate. Although they seem justified within each respective paradigm, the reactions feed on each other in a continuing and unresolvable cycle.

To break out of such cycles before people rigidly entrench themselves in positions that caricature their underlying concern, we can leap to a higher level of logic, a "both/and" logic, and deal with difficulties by means of a mutually empowering style of leadership. For example, Pastor Bill's authority as a teacher is well accepted in the congregation. He often helps members identify the basic paradigm they assume and talk about the difference it makes in interpreting behaviors. They proceed to evaluate the situation or negotiate the disagreement, searching for a solution that embraces all the concerns expressed. In this kind of leadership, pastors and executive officers are truly authorized and empowered to lead and to draw boundaries but are not authorized to exercise control beyond stated limits. They are not authorized to use domination tactics.

In the logic of the new paradigm, power is derived not from one's position in a hierarchy or by one's exercise of top-down control but by service in a coordinating role within a web of people in partnership. This approach demands a greater variety and flexibility of strategies ("maneuverability") for problem solving. From such a nexus leaders can orchestrate synergy and power sharing fairly and appropriately so that power is not an either/or phenomenon.

Three Temptations

Paradox has always been woven into the warp and woof of the human condition. To have the capacity to imagine and accomplish great things and yet to be limited by weakness, sin, lack of knowledge, and death is ironic and painfully paradoxical. Three temptations in the human situation are especially alluring in religious contexts: the temptation to assume our predictions as facts, the temptation to deny and disrespect ambiguity, and the temptation to express this denial and disrespect by seeking or claiming logical and absolute truth.[1] These temptations draw us into totalisms and set the stage for double binds.

We are frequently tempted, for example, to believe that our predictions are unshakable fact and to use our capacity for prediction to calm our anxieties and enlarge our egos. Sometimes we put people into rigid roles and stereotypes, as if they were totally predictable. We put them in a crazy-making bind that forces them to choose either to please us by living up to these predictions, thus sacrificing their freedom, or to act freely and risk offending us.

We are also tempted to use our capacity for prediction and control to dominate experiences—such as our own emotions and bodily functions or the thoughts and feelings of another person—though these cannot be predicted or controlled with certainty. These efforts put us in dilemmas, such as having to fight one's body or nature to take care of oneself or having to accept psychological invasion to receive another's love.

In addition, our human situation leads us into paradoxical binds because of the ambiguity of communication and of human relationships. Because words and nonverbal messages can send contradictory messages, the possibilities for confusion are endless. We set up a further bind if we try to eliminate all ambiguity and insist on total clarity. A degree of clarity—clarifying expectations or naming a dilemma—may be helpful. But if we try to squeeze all the ambiguity out of richly multi-layered and complex human relationships, we choke life and create binds in which emotion cannot flow.

Closely related to the attempt to deny ambiguity, the human penchant to seek absolute truth leads us into many paradoxes. Such certainty not only is impossible; it strips people, nature, and God (i.e., life itself) of the very mysteries, uncertainties, and surprises that keep us human and God divine, and keep life exciting. It solves our anxieties about uncertainty at far too high a price. Shall we sell our souls to purchase safety? If we seek so to save our lives, we will lose them.

Totalism in the Church

We are often especially tempted to seek special prediction, deny ambiguity, and claim absolute truth in religion. Congregations become fertile ground for pathogenic paradoxes. When people come demanding, "Tell us the life-giving truth, but make sure it is absolute so that our deepest anxieties about uncertainty can be controlled," leaders are in a bind. People can become anxious and angry if told that part of the life-giving truth is that we must live with shades gray and that the more we study Scripture and mature in faith, the more shades of gray we see. We have no access to absolute truth. Rather, Truth (God) has access to us, and God's truth is not as fixed and predictable as the word "absolute" would suggest. This kind of truth taps anxiety and anger in those who expect religion to ease their discomfort.

Pastor Jill was asked by a member of a study group what Scripture says about abortion. She answered that Scripture does not discuss the issue directly and that we need to apply scriptural teachings such as the value of life, the dignity of persons, and our role as covenant people to make up our own minds on this difficult issue. The questioner was upset by the answer. He said little in response to the pastor, but he began telling others that Pastor Jill was a pro-choice feminist who did not believe in scriptural truth. Jill sensed that she was in a bind but could not get the man to talk about it. If she told the truth, the credibility of her leadership would be damaged. If she hedged her teaching, how could she feel that she was being faithful?

Our social context, meanwhile, seduces us to deny our limits. Advances in science and technology, the exponential increase of information, and the global triumph of capitalism have pushed the limits of our analysis, prediction, reach, control, and possession so far that we are tempted to deny limits altogether. The old paradigm fosters this denial. We fail to see how more analysis, prediction, reach, control, and possession could create a problem because we believe that having more of these is the solution. All around us people feel in their bodies, emotions, relationships, and spirits the draining and battering effects of daily life and work in a society that denies its limits and punishes them if they do not acquiesce in the denial. Many turn to alcohol, drugs, addictive relationships, work addictions, obsessive pursuit of possessions, and entertainment to dull pain and keep anxiety at bay.

Many of these emotionally and spiritually battered people are seeking to meet their emotional needs and to find spiritual solutions to the pathogenic binds created by the denial of limits or by faulty solutions in other parts of society. They come seeking healing and empowerment. Sometimes they seek it, or the congregation offers it, through flawed solutions that duplicate widespread attempted solutions in society—black-and-white answers, unlimited growth, domination and victory, or simply more busywork or more fund raising as solutions to deeper problems. Such solutions leave members even more deeply stuck and dissatisfied, perhaps without knowing why. They may in turn blame the pastor or congregation for not meeting their needs.

The combination of such demands and expectations of the congregation or its leaders creates a climate of paradoxical binds for the pastor and leaders that will almost surely bring out the church's and pastor's worst and result in disillusionment for all.

Limits, Choices, Acceptance

How can we escape this climate? The paths out require recognition of
greater complexity and choices, as well as acceptance of limitations and
of life's painful but unavoidable paradoxes. Totalisms involve the assumption of illegitimate totalities—trying to put everything in one box
to overcome paradox. The opposite is to assert "legitimate partialities"—
to accept limits, imperfections, incompleteness, and life's difficult paradoxes. To put it theologically, a climate of grace that paradoxically
accepts us despite our limitations unlocks the paradoxical binds and
stuck points, freeing the creative flow of God's life and love through us.

A major role of both pastoral and lay leadership is to empathize
with both unavoidable and avoidable paradoxes and to define limits that
help overcome the avoidable ones. Leaders should articulate the totalistic expectations that members have of their leaders and that leaders have
of themselves. Second, leaders should sit down together and hammer out
contracts or "covenants" that express "legitimate partialities"[2]—i.e.,
concrete goals and limits for each leader, for the leadership group, and
for the congregation. These goals should not only provide a significant
focus but should also clarify how much is enough and how much depends on the help of others. Third, lay leaders should recognize that
emotionally needy people are drawn increasingly to religious contexts
and that leaders must make sure that the pastor and staff are protected,
by clear boundaries and other emotional supports, from the binds that
will inevitably arise in dealing with such people.

In many effective pastor/leader teams the members demarcate limits
about what is reasonable and healthy to expect, particularly for the pastor, and educate the congregation about the need to support these limits.
One pastor I know sits down with leaders to discuss the coming year's
priorities. Their discussion notes what will have to be slighted or left
undone to fulfill these priorities. The outcome of this negotiation is an-
nounced to the members. This simple and healthy limit-setting process
can prevent many confused expectations. It is an irony of life that the
sincere message to "go slow," to "focus," to "just be there," to "stop
trying to change," and to "acknowledge limits" helps both congregations
and leaders to become more productive and spiritual.

Finally, to put it in plain language, unless we can learn to be limited
human beings together, laughing, crying, playing, fighting, struggling,

and empathizing with each other's dilemmas, we will make each other miserable with crazy-making paradoxes as we try to be "religious" and "righteous." Rather than trying to transform each other into "better Christians," and trying to make our religion solve unsolvable difficulties, we can learn together to live with these difficulties humanly and humanely.

Questions

1. Give examples of conflicting expectations and either/or thinking in your congregation that puts leaders or other members in paradoxical binds.

2. What are you doing in your congregation (naming, humor, acknowledging limits) to help humanize the inescapable paradoxes your pastor and leaders face?

3. What factors in society and religion increase the likelihood of a totalistic emotional climate and therefore of double binds?

4. What are you doing to counter the destructive paradoxes your leaders face?

CHAPTER 6

Mishandled Conflict

Perhaps the most widely mishandled difficulty of all is conflict. Conflict may be difficult and painful, but in most cases it is not a problem until it is mishandled.

Utopian Syndrome and Conflict

While problems in mishandling conflict are prevalent in American culture, they are particularly common in Christian congregations because of the loss of understanding of their Hebraic roots and because of the utopianism that tends to accompany our expectations of religion, the church, and pastors. The church, we believe, should have no disagreement or political struggle and definitely no anger!

Unfortunately, such a conflict-free milieu does not exist in the church or elsewhere—nor should it. A world with no conflict would preclude much of our struggle for integrity and authenticity in relationships and limit the depth of spiritual growth. Utopianism gives rise to problems when directed toward a pastor or other church leader, or by them toward the congregation as a whole.

One pastor expressed irritation at a woman for her bothersome remark at a board meeting. He later apologized, but she refused to accept the apology. Instead, regarding her actions as "biblical," she brought both the current and the past president of the congregation to support her as she berated him as a "bad pastor" for displaying anger or irritation on more than one occasion. This, she said, was unacceptable behavior from a pastor. She was unwilling to accept his apology, let alone acknowledge that she had played any part in the problem. The president said,

"The pastor has apologized. He's a human being too. Don't you think he is entitled to a bad day now and then?" As simple and obvious as this intervention sounds, the pastor later said these were among the most healing and freeing words ever uttered on his behalf.

Being allowed to be human and to voice angry feelings now and then helped him feel less frustrated and irritable. It even helped him take a sympathetic view of the way events in this woman's life had shaped her reactions. If we give people, including pastors and other church leaders, space to be human, with feelings and imperfections, they tend to act more like the human beings God meant them to be. But if we scrutinize their faults under a magnifying glass, these traits become more obvious. If we expect them to be more than human, they may respond with less than healthy humanness.

Theological perspective is an important consideration. The Bible does not assume that chaos, anger, and conflict are always evil or that their total absence is ideal. Keep in mind the story of God's wrestlings with Israel and human sin and especially the cross. It is understatement to say that conflict plays a crucial role in God's creating, calling, healing, saving involvement with creation. While much anger and conflict grow out of sin or lead to sin in our lives, neither anger nor conflict is necessarily sinful. As the Apostle Paul advises, "Be angry but do not sin; do not let the sun go down on your anger, and do not make room for the devil" (Eph. 4:26-27).

The vision of God that grows from the old paradigm, and the versions of religion that express it, have little place for such an involved and vulnerable God or for a lifestyle that is similarly vulnerable and involved. In the old-paradigm vision, God either stands aloof from all conflict or crushes it victoriously. Little room is left for the possibility of anger without sin. The old-paradigm vision sees anger and conflict as leading in one of only two directions—toward destruction or domination. These cultural assumptions are reinforced by our own experiences of destructive conflict. Ironically, many of our experiences with anger and conflict are destructive precisely because our fears and beliefs lead us to mishandle them. We create self-fulfilling prophecies.

In our paranoia about conflict, we not only fight our opponents; we also fight anger and conflict. While both may be temporarily restrained, neither is a defeatable foe. If we do not make friends, or at least cautious allies, with anger and conflict, our efforts to escape or defeat them will prevent their accomplishing potentially healthy purposes. The only way to win in the long run with our opponents, our angers, and our conflicts is to make them our friends, do what we can to "love our enemies," and use them for constructive purposes—or at least turn their energies judo-style to our own defense and purpose.

Our fears of anger and conflict result in a lack of positive experiences with conflict resolution or constructive channeling of angry feelings. Consequently, we (and I can speak only from experience among Christians) develop few individual and institutional skills for handling conflict constructively. This failure is unfortunate for the church's mission in a violence-ridden world. How can we in the church help the world learn to fight fair and reconcile if we cannot learn to fight like Christians in the church?

Constructive Anger and Conflict

When anger and aggression are channeled constructively, these energies help us mark our boundaries, define our identities, motivate our actions, clarify vulnerable feelings, and assert ourselves. As such, they play a crucial role in our emotional health and maturation. Take away anger/aggression, and you remove one of the drives that help make us who we are. When we try to deny, suppress, dominate, or abolish anger, we miss out on its positive potential. What's more, unacknowledged anger can, from its place in hiding, twist our behavior and distort even our best intentions.

The unexamined and unchecked drive toward togetherness and supposed love can undermine human dignity and identity formation more subtly than unchecked emotional separation. Emotions and behaviors we tend to idealize in the church—love, concern, caring, closeness, and protectiveness—can in reality be a mixture of love and aggression. Labels and conscious good intentions may mask anger, hatred, fear, arrogance, and emotional imperialism. When we suppress awareness of our aggressive side, the other more appealing emotions seduce us into believing that we are unambiguously righteous, confuse our sense of appropriate boundaries and limits, and stunt our growth.

It is more comfortable to believe that our motives are unambiguously good. Who, for example, wants to admit that when expressing concern for his pastor or for recipients of his charity, he might also be angry and scared because the pastor's message or the presence of oppressed groups threatens his justification for possessing wealth and privilege? Who wants to admit that she is being kind to someone partly to keep that person indebted and under control?

Conversely, it is not only expressions of love, closeness, and belonging that serve mental health. Drawing boundaries (i.e., saying "no" and "not me"), separating, asserting, and expressing anger responsibly can help solidify identity and contribute to healthy relationships.

Functional Fights

Nor are all congregational fights to be deplored. Some recurring fights serve a systemic function which the system and its members do not know how to fulfill any other way—creating intensity or increasing distance in overinvolved relationships. To see this useful conflict as a problem and remove it without providing people a better way to meet the need may result in worse problems. Removing such conflict can be like Jesus' story of casting out one demon and leaving an inner spiritual vacuum that is filled by seven new demons.

Holy Family Church's core was made up of an extended clan marked by a major split that had existed for years. The friendly conflict expressed itself through an ongoing argument about whether the congregation's giving should focus on local or more distant mission. Pastor Gil tried to settle the argument by explaining why the "distant mission" side was biblically correct. This explanation silenced the debate on the surface, but the rejected group went underground with its views and began subtly resisting and undermining Gil's pastoral work. Meanwhile, the favored group became increasingly prideful and gained more power in the church's formal organizations. As a result, the two sides became more alienated than ever, both in the congregation and in everyday life. The old argument had served some positive purposes. Members could have been taught to disagree respectfully and still carry on this debate to keep alive a certain creative tension. Instead, the attempted removal of the conflict upset the balance and left a partial vacuum.

Another reason to see fights in a positive light and to quit trying to solve them is this: Relationships from which aggression is excluded remain superficial. Like poorly chewed and digested food, they do not supply full nourishment. Congregations that do not know how to affirm and hear anger, how to set up "safe" rules and structures of conflict and to make sure everyone fights fair, have relationships stuck in superficiality.

Healthy conflict helps us clarify our identity as individuals and as congregations. If we as God's people cannot say who we are *not*, we are unlikely to be able to say who we *are*. We are unlikely to focus on effective goals, roles, and targets for mission and ministry. We are unlikely to discipline our group to eliminate behavior and processes destructive to the whole. Healthy conflict is not only possible but essential.

Mishandled Offense and Reconciliation

Some conflict can be constructively handled by educating people about its positive potential and training them in conflict management and resolution. However, significant sins are usually involved in any situation we recognize as a congregational conflict, and the approach we need is that of seeking authentic reconciliation. Reconciliation after a hurt or offense is to the congregation and larger religious groupings what blood circulation and healing of a wound are to the body. If the body did not have self-healing capability, even small wounds would be life-threatening. Wounds must be cleaned, painful though that be, or they will heal incompletely, become infected, and lead to more acute pain and peril later. If an emotional wound is covered over too quickly without being cleaned out thoroughly by grief work, infection will set in and lead to bitterness, depression, physical disease, violence, or other relational problems. These can spread and infect a whole group as destructive emotional triangles multiply. The solution becomes the problem. The same is true in regard to cutting off circulation. In extreme cases, a tourniquet is a temporary solution. But if blood flow is cut off for too long, there can be no healing. A limb may be lost.

Sins must be admitted, honest regret expressed, and forgiveness extended. One-sided blaming must be set aside. In most cases, confession and forgiveness must be mutual for true reconciliation. People must look to shared responsibility to negotiate new solutions and relationships. And we must try not to achieve reconciliation by teaching, shaming, or forcing others into denial of their anger or into quick and easy forgiveness. We must hear and acknowledge the others' feelings, respond to their needs appropriately, and give them time and space to come to a genuine forgiveness of the heart.

Mishandling Offenses

Offenses, like other difficulties, can be mishandled by Terrible Simplification, by the Utopia Syndrome, or by addressing the offense or reconciliation at the wrong logical or systemic level. An example of a wrong logical level is an effort to make what can occur only spontaneously (e.g., forgiveness and healing) happen on command. The Utopia Syndrome can be illustrated by a church that creates problems by trying to resolve personality differences or tensions with which they simply need to learn to live graciously and with humor. For example, it is not realistic to expect every member to like a given pastor (or vice versa), and the attempt can lead not only to a lack of humor but to more serious problems.

Most often, I suspect, Terrible Simplification (seeing no problem where there is one) takes place as we deny that an offense occurred when it did. For example: Someone says he has been hurt or offended by another; the other tells him he should not feel this way because he was not wronged. In counseling, I make distinctions among the levels of facts, feelings, and interpretations and establish a rule that if someone feels offended, she has a right to have her feelings taken seriously. No one has a right to tell another family member or congregation member what she should feel or to ignore her feelings. This does not mean that the "facts" can ever be sorted out with any certainty or that the listener must agree with the speaker's interpretation of the event. It is quite another matter, after feelings are taken seriously, to sort out whether sins may have been committed that require apology, forgiveness, and commitment to behavioral change. It is more difficult to get such healthy rules for a relationship accepted within a board or community, but pastors and leaders can make progress toward such acceptance if they agree on the rules and work together to establish them before a crisis.

As with grief, shutting down someone's feelings of hurt in the congregation is like covering over a wound too quickly without cleansing it thoroughly. The wound does not automatically heal with time. Infection will set in and lead to problems that can spread and infect the whole congregation. If we are not open with people or groups that we feel have wronged us, or if they are not willing to work for reconciliation when we openly share the hurt, the healing process is cut off. Infection sets in most often as we share our hurt and anger with others, attempting to win their sympathy and salve our pain by urging them to reinforce our self-righteous perspective. As people are triangled emotionally into protecting us or helping us wreak revenge, triangles multiply in the emotional system like infectious bacteria multiplying in a wound. Cleaning out wounds and restoring circulation are essential to healing both the grief of loss and the pain of broken relationships.

From a systemic viewpoint, emotional and spiritual wounds occur and circulation is cut off not only in individuals but also in groups and at the "in-betweens" of relationships. Congregations and larger religious structures sin, are sinned against, and need to practice confession and reconciliation. Indeed, a congregation where this work is not taking place with much regularity is like a body with little healing circulation of blood.

For congregations to get unstuck, they need frequent confession, forgiveness, and reconciliation taking place at a variety of in-between points—one-to-one between individual members, between pastors and individuals, between pastors and the congregation, between pastors and boards, between congregations and individuals, between congregational groups and members, between local and denominational church systems, and between larger religious groups such as Christians and Jews. Operating out of the highly individualistic assumptions of our culture, most of us tend to be blinded to our participation in systemic sin and to our need to participate in confession, forgiveness, and reconciliation as part of, or in relation to, corporate groups. We also tend to run short on useful concepts, practical techniques, and rituals for this kind of reconciliation work. How can we remedy this deficiency?

- Recognize the need to work toward corporate reconciliation at the congregation's in-between points.
- Do not force or rush forgiveness.
- Establish procedures and rules, and appoint referees for fair fighting in the congregation.
- Approach sins and offenses at the appropriate systemic levels.

Forgiveness or Reconciliation?

Reconciliation seems to be a more systemic concept than forgiveness.
Sometimes the biblical notion of forgiveness is simply ripped out of the
context of God's desire for restoring justice and peace in broken relationships. Granted, forgiveness can be one-sided and lead to healing for
one party in a broken relationship. One-sided forgiveness can sometimes
lead also to reconciliation of the relationship, as when God first forgives
us. But with human relationships, offenses are seldom one-sided. In most
cases, if reconciliation is to take place, if the full, healing circulation of
life and love is to be restored in the corporate religious body, confession
and forgiveness must be mutual. People must hear and acknowledge
each other's feelings and legitimate rights and take shared responsibility
to negotiate new relationships if reconciliation is to take place.

     We ought to seek reconciliation in the congregation, unless we must
forgo this ideal for the sake of safety or to achieve justice, as in the case
of certain criminal acts. Then, an internal and one-sided forgiveness
may be the healthiest realistic option, even as we distance ourselves or
pursue legal or protective action.

Reconciling Individuals and Groups

Steps toward seeking reconciliation with a board or a whole congregation can be difficult to identify for the individual, as for the group seeking reconciliation with an individual. Congregations and their boards
often do not understand themselves as systemic entities that can sin as
well as confess, repent, absolve, and work toward reconciliation. How
do you get a group's attention or confront a system with its sins against
you? How does a system confess or apologize? And how does an individual apologize to a group? Boards are sometimes unsure of their corporate identity or responsibility, or seek to disown it.

     The legitimate roles of elected officials in handling complaints and
offenses are not always clear and explicit. We could do much to help
people feel reconciled with their congregations by clarifying openly who
is authorized to field complaints and within what rules of behavior. Assuming that complainants are always innocent victims and will behave
maturely and fairly without clear, enforced rules of procedure is as naïve

as assuming that complainants are always troublemakers. Either approach can turn difficulties into problems.

We need rules requiring people to state the specific wrong they suffered, what redress they seek, and what behavioral change they ask of the offender. Those who bring complaints should be held accountable for any part they played in the problem and any sins of gossip or triangling of others they committed out of anger or hurt feelings. They should be held objectively accountable through neutral witnesses (as in Matthew 18) for taking adequate steps to work out the problem directly with the pastor or other leader, unless crime or personal danger is a factor. The elected officials who hear the complaints may need to take an active role in monitoring and mediating the process fairly and in refusing to take complaints seriously unless the complainant accepts the due-process rules.

Sometimes reconciliation between an individual and a congregation can be furthered through rituals or symbolic gestures—such as a board's giving a card, a gift, a salary increase, or a special invitation to the individual or by the individual's making a similar gesture to the group. Symbols, rituals, words, or actions that are meant as an apology are rich with ambiguity and can often be more powerful than an explicit verbal apology. However, ambiguous symbolic gestures may also be misunderstood or miss their mark. Consequently, they may best be used to prepare the way for a more direct approach rather than as a substitute.

Sometimes, to define exactly whom or what we are addressing, we need to clearly identify our intended audience: "I want to address this board [congregation, group] as a responsible whole with the intent to try to work this out," or "I want to speak on behalf of this board to the complainant." Then the work of confronting, apologizing, and reconciling can proceed. After receiving feedback on how our effort is received, we may need to try a different tack.

Unless you are exceptionally charming and able, as one pastor put it, to "tell people to go to hell in such a way that they look forward to the trip," I do not recommend trying to criticize, confront, and wrestle a confession or statement of repentance from a board or larger group. Any approach perceived as a threat will trigger the group's homeostatic forces.

If a wronged individual tries to initiate discussion of the group's sin, the system, as well as the individuals in it, can be elusive. Defense mechanisms of individuals and the group can collude. Opinions and reactions can be split. Responsibility can fall in the cracks as some members remain silent or withdraw. Responsibility can easily be denied and blame turned on the one who appears to be angry or attacking. Individuals who readily speak to others outside of the meeting may refrain from speaking up in the meeting. Without clearly established rules to hold each other accountable, group members who feel anxiety in the group will often prefer to speak in private outside the meeting. In this way, power-moves, emotional triangles, secrets, and distortions can multiply without accountability and continue to wound and undermine the spirit of the group. We as leaders need to help congregational groups claim their responsibility and avoid the multiplication of such triangles.

Despite seemingly stubborn reactions, group identity can be fragile and group spirit vulnerable. It is questionable how much true confession and reconciliation can be accomplished with people or groups that do not know who they are or are easily threatened. Any invitation to reconciliation should follow the gentle spirit of Jesus, who though assertive, did not, Isaiah 42 tells us, "break a bruised reed" or "quench a dimly burning wick." Get the group's attention as a responsible entity and "join" with it, for example, by reminding it of its mission or of good works God has done through it and the ways the members have worked as a team using the variety of their gifts. Then make honest and heartfelt "I" statements about what has hurt you, how you believe it has hurt their mission and your ability to work together, and what you hope can be different. Then let the Holy Spirit take care of the rest.

Insofar as possible, pastors or leaders can also accomplish much in relation to the group as a whole by working their way (openly, not secretly) person by person and family by family through the entire board or congregation to discuss an issue or build understanding and work toward reconciliation.

Since time and energy are limited, energy may be focused in two ways. First (perhaps with the help of a spiritual director or counselor), be intentional in working on your relationship with the person in the congregation with whom you have an unreconciled, stuck relationship. I do not suggest trying to overcome every difference of personality or philosophy with such members but rather working toward a mutual understanding and respectful acceptance. Sometimes in family therapy I find it most revealing and efficient to ask who it is in the family system with whom each client lacks a good relationship, and to focus attention precisely at these points. Usually key issues will converge and emerge in these relationships, and any progress made there will reverberate powerfully throughout the system. The same can be true in congregations.

Second, the pastor or lay leader may determine who plays key roles in the emotional system and focus reconciliation efforts on representative persons or subgroups (such as symbolic parents, protectors of tradition, gatekeepers). Research, observation, study of the congregation's history, and "asking around" may be required to discover who these emotionally significant people are, but it will be worth the effort. Once you learn which spokespeople represent the congregation's emotional system (not necessarily the formal leaders), attempt to gain their understanding and support. Sometimes reconciliation with people in key roles in the emotional system serves to address the system as a whole. It may also be helpful for these informal leaders to encourage and "unofficially authorize" official leaders to speak on behalf of the group.

The Need for Corporate Confession

Whether they are unofficially authorized by the leaders of the emotional system or not, I would like to see official leaders more often set an example by leading others in corporate confession, apology, and reconciliation efforts. How much stuckness could be overcome if leaders more often asked on behalf of their congregation or denomination for the forgiveness of other churches and groups of people against whom they have sinned? How much healing might occur if congregational boards apologized and sought to make things right when they have failed to support their pastor adequately? How much love and teamwork might result if pastors apologized publicly for not caring properly for the spirit of a congregation? This is not to say that confession completes the hard work of reconciliation, but it gives it a kick-start.

If congregations and groups of members learned to confess corporate sins committed against a pastor or leader, such confession could help them get unstuck.

Can Forgiveness Be Demanded?

Failure to accept responsibility and to confess group sin can lead to
blaming the "unforgiving" victim. Such blaming often attempts to solve
the problem at the wrong logical level and thus creates paradoxes that
make the problem worse.

Pastor Sue felt she had been sinned against by her congregation's
council. The experience was painful, and each time she aired hurt or
anger, it seemed to go unheard. Either none of the members perceived it
as their role to speak on behalf of the council, or no one perceived that
any corporate sin had been committed. The more Sue felt unheard, the
more hurt, frustrated, and angry she became. Eventually the executive
board offered her its solution. They demanded that she forgive and let
go of her feelings and not talk about them again. She became more angry at their inability to hear her feelings, to express corporate repentance, and to make amends. They pushed their demand further, with
condescending lectures about the importance of forgiveness. The council would admit no wrong on its part. Everything was in the past, the
officers said, and the fact that Pastor Sue still wanted to talk about it
showed that she was unforgiving. Athough Sue now felt even more furi-
ous, she restrained her anger and backed off.

Nearing a point of desperation, Sue risked becoming particularly
assertive with the executive officers. When she insisted that they listen
to her concerns or she would not cease to confront them, they asked in
surprise, "What in the world could we have done differently?" Apparently they felt they had tried hard and yet remained oblivious to their
failings as a council. At this point the pastor began to speak, and for the
first time they seemed to listen.

Their attempts to coerce her to forgive and forget created destructive paradoxes for her (e.g., forgoing justice and reconciliation in order
to be considered a true Christian). When they started to listen and
understand that they had been at fault and needed to do things differently in the future, this event released the paradoxical bind and allowed
reconciliation, not only between individuals but also between the pastor
and the council as a whole. I do not recommend this strategy in every
situation. But for this pastor, who tended to bite her lip and then occasionally get in power struggles she could not win, assertive persistence
with the executive committee in private was the solution needed.

As this story demonstrates, congregational leaders can aggravate a problem in their attempts to deal with someone who feels offended if they demand she forgive or let go of her anger. The demand need not be direct. We can shame and pressure people with "dirty looks," innuendoes, or other nonverbal messages. Indeed, such messages are inevitable if we believe that anger is equivalent to a lack of forgiveness, that anger is sinful, or that "good Christians" hurt by others should simply "forgive and forget."

I am not suggesting that forgiveness and reconciliation have no elements of decision. But these are not simple, quick decisions that immediately solve everything, nor are they decisions others can make for us. Attempts to persuade others to let go of anger or to forgive prematurely are forms of Terrible Simplification that minimize both the seriousness of sin and the painful complexity of the process of forgiveness. These attempts often produce a result opposite from the one we want.

Even when the individual agrees with the demand to forgive and tries to make it happen, the result is a Terrible Simplification. Forgiveness cannot be forced by an act of will or by pressure. Trying to forgive and forget often prevents our healing enough to truly forgive and forget. Attempting to force forgiveness is an action at the wrong level of strategy. Such attempts put us in binding paradoxes in which (1) we must deny our sense of justice and our true feelings, and (2) we try to force and control a healing process that largely can occur only spontaneously. The more this solution is pressed upon us, the more stuck we are between impossible choices, and the more slowly we heal.

Forgiveness as Grief Work

Forgiveness is to be encouraged and held as an ideal, but trying to force it or demand it too quickly short-circuits the healing process. Forgiveness is a grief process involving pain, loss, and anger, as well as a mix of other intense emotions such as guilt, shame, fear, helplessness, and deep sadness. Grief processes take much more time than our culture typically allows. Healthy grief processes move forward but continue in some form throughout our lives. Grief takes work. It takes pain. We must stay with terrifying and agonizing emotions long enough to let them have their say and mean what they mean. This process may include conveying the significance of the offense or the importance of making changes in our lives to seek greater justice or wholeness in response to the offense.

Often it takes much talk to wrest meaning from the grief before one can reconstitute a sense of integrity and selfhood strong enough to forgive in a healthy, authentic way. This is especially true after a person's boundaries have been transgressed or the spirit has been violated. It simply adds insult to injury when we demand total forgiveness before a person is emotionally ready.

Of course, we can decide to forgive and say we have forgiven to look good to ourselves or others or to bring quick closure to something so painful we would rather avoid it. This route, however, does not often lead to a forgiveness of the heart. We can choose to undergo such an arduous grief process and bring closure to it after the healing process is well along. But this is far different from forcing ourselves to forgive and forget. Such a glib demand grows out of a control-based paradigm that believes people should be individualistic and rational "captains of their souls" in total command of their bodies through their wills. Real emotional beings cannot fit into this kind of box without doing violence to their souls and distorting their humanity.

A Case of Anger as a Solution

Not only is it usually counterproductive to demand forgiveness, but sometimes it is most productive to restrain the effort to forgive too quickly. A memorable case during my training in family therapy involved a woman whose son was abusing drugs and ignoring her rules. Our therapy team soon learned that she had been gang-raped several years earlier, and she felt that her unhealed anger had something to do with her parenting problems. After more inquiry, we discovered that she had been to several therapists, each of whom had told her that anger was at the root of her problems and that she must learn to let go of it and forgive. The fact was that she had tried to forgive, and had not succeeded in doing so. After more discussion with the woman and the therapeutic team, we decided to reverse the prescription. We told her she must definitely not forgive or let go of her anger yet. Not only was her anger appropriate to the terrible evil that had been done to her, we explained, but also she needed the anger. She needed angry energy to build her self-esteem, to assert herself as a parent, and to work to right injustices like the one done to her.

This intervention was the turning point in her therapy. Her mood and self-esteem improved. She took a volunteer job helping rape victims. She became more assertive in parenting. The problems with her son eased dramatically. She had been freed from a paradoxical trap within a few sessions. She seemed able to let go of the destructive side of the anger that caused problems. Forgiveness can free us and humanize us when we freely choose to do the grief work to seek the miracle of healing. When we turn forgiveness into a demand, we create paradoxes that get us stuck. When we affirm anger and the drive toward justice, we often free people from both the need for revenge and the trap of pretense.

Fair Fighting: Rules and Referees

The guidelines Jesus gives in Matthew 18:15-17, used in the spirit of its biblical context, can, with minor modifications, provide a workable set of rules and point to referees for fair fighting. This Scripture text says to go first directly to the person who has hurt you and try to resolve the issue privately. If that person will not listen, take one or two witnesses and try again. Jesus then says, if the offender still will not listen, take it to the church.

Perhaps Jesus meant literally to bring the issue to the whole gathered congregation. It seems within the spirit of these guidelines to add the possibility of steps that involve increasingly higher levels of complexity and forcefulness—going to a personnel committee, then to the congregational officers, then to a congregational meeting. If the individuals still will not listen, even to the congregation, then treat them as outsiders to the community ("Let such a one be to you as a Gentile and a tax collector" [Matt. 18:17b]).

Judging by this passage and the words of Paul in 1 Corinthians 5, and 2 Thessalonians 3:14-15, the early church was expected to apply strong measures in the case of blatant unrepentance after such processes were completed. The biblical texts stand in sharp contrast to many congregations today whose level of expectation and group discipline seems to be lower than that of many social clubs. When congregations do occasionally get serious about disciplining an unrepentant member, they often have no clarity about this text and no established structure for ensuring that the steps are executed rightly.

Note several points about these guidelines. First, this text addresses the need to confront clear, one-sided, sinful offenses, although the general model could be applied to perceived offenses that need to be aired and sorted out. Even in the case of a clear-cut offense, however, the text does not say to take one or two people who will side with you and increase the pressure. The people who go along with the offended person are supposed to act as witnesses to give an objective report. In cases where the issue has to do with sins on both sides or misunderstandings or disagreements, witnesses are needed to ensure a fair and healthy process, not to help one side pressure the other.

Secondly, as can be noted from the immediate and broader context of Matthew 18 and the Pauline passages cited above, these steps are commended in the environment of a loving, forgiving community of faith. They are taken not for retribution but for correction and reconciliation, the protection of the congregation, and the ultimate salvation of the offender.

Third, few of us have the patience and courage to work stepwise so long and patiently to handle a difficulty. Few of us are willing to prepare our own hearts rightly before we confront another. We want quick, easy solutions, so we often short-circuit the process by leaving out the stronger steps, or we jump too quickly to a higher level, even when we think we are following biblical guidelines.

Fourth, these guidelines acknowledge the need to summon more help and, eventually, more forcefulness under certain circumstances. We in the church cannot afford to be naïve about mental illness and evil among our membership and in ourselves. For the sake of the faithful community as well as our clergy, we must build in safeguards to protect them from the pathology and evil that may arise in us and among us. And we must protect our members from the potential pathology and evil of leaders.

To provide such protection, leaders need to make clear rules and limits about acceptable behavior toward one another. Some rules can be stated clearly in by-laws and policy statements. Other rules need to be laid out in the form of a positive vision statement and negotiated at meetings and in informal relationships on an ongoing basis. The mental health field, under the guidance of our biblical traditions, can help us clarify healthy rules of relationship, such as the right to feel and have those feelings recognized, the right to boundaries and space to be yourself and to hold your views, the right to impact others meaningfully, the right to know information that affects you, and the right to have power and authority commensurate with the responsibilities given to you.

It is probably most effective to negotiate such rules in a structured retreat or meeting involving formal and informal congregational leaders and perhaps an outside resource person whose suggestions will be respected by all. Most important in this process is that the rules be discussed widely and publicly in the congregation, and that members agree to hold each other accountable to the agreement reached.

Once we agree to such rules, we also must be ready to use power for respectful discipline of those who refuse to play by the rules. If we are not organized and ready for such discipline, then manipulative, sick, or evil members will hold the congregation hostage. These individuals will confuse systemic levels, use contradictory multilevel communication, manipulate well-meaning people, play people off against each other, draw in higher-than-needed levels of power or authority to get their way, and generally use illegitimate and psychologically complex strategies to tie the congregation in knots. Even previously healthy members may get so caught up in the frustration of dealing with manipulative people that they become unhealthy and do their own leaping to higher or inappropriate levels at the expense of the group's well-being.

We might be better able to follow Jesus' guidelines if we developed our skills and structures at each subsystem of the guidelines. This means bringing in or identifying internal resource people and designing coursework and events for all ages. People would be trained and encouraged to confront each other, in the case of an offense, with gentleness. A gentle confrontation is not to be understood as conflict avoidance or weak passivity but as humble, loving, Christlike boldness. At the second level of these guidelines from Jesus, we might do well to appoint and train members who could go along with others and take the role of witness (and perhaps referee). Because of the inexperience of our congregations in applying the third step in church discipline, "Take it to the church," we may need creative new approaches to apply this step in a realistic way. Use of structured "Group Conferences" is one possibility.

Group Conferences for Church Discipline

A slight modification of Jesus' guidelines would apply what is known in the field of criminal justice as the "family group conference method." This model borrows from and modifies methods used by indigenous peoples of New Zealand. A leader coordinates meetings in which the offender is surrounded by family and friends, as well as by the victim and the victim's family. "Reintegrative shame" is used, confronting the offender with the pain and anger of the offended as well as of the two families involved.

The hoped-for result is remorse and behavioral change that will allow the offender to be reintegrated into the family and community. The method has proved powerful. In some ways it parallels the call to repentance and reconciliation in the religious community. Congregations could modify this model for group discipline—for use especially in instances when people generate so much power by their offending behavior that they hold the group emotionally captive.

This method would give the congregation the kind of loving "clout" needed to deal with the increasing challenge of emotionally manipulative and character-disordered individuals. The method would also give us a much-needed additional level of the system at which to deal with offenses. This level is higher in complexity and inclusiveness than the one-to-one and the "bring-one-or-two-witnesses-along" steps in Matthew and less complex and inclusive than taking it to the whole congregation. This approach also involves the people closest to the problem rather than board members, who represent the congregation but may lack the first-hand information or motivation to invest the required time and emotional energy to sort things out.

Rules for conflict resolution sessons in any effort to confront offenses, it is helpful for a congregation to clarify and agree ahead of time on rules and limits of acceptable behavior. Often, for reconciliation to be complete, a safe systemic context is needed in which to wrestle things out. Most issues of hurt or offense are not clear-cut, and grappling with each other's thoughts and feelings can help to sort them out. We often need a gifted third person to set up rules for a level playing field and to referee confrontations so that no one is allowed to fight dirty. This pattern of solution is one that many congregations have not tried when they are stuck. I believe stuckness could frequently be overcome if we invited in skilled mediators or if we trained individuals to set forth rules and to referee sessions of fair fighting and conflict resolution—especially if all the pertinent individuals were included openly in the mediated sessions.

Well-known rules used by family therapists in conflicts and confrontations include:

- Make sure you as a helper do not take sides emotionally but can see both points of view. This caution does not mean one should excuse wrongs or have no opinions about right and wrong. It simply means to recognize the complexity and ambiguity of relationships, that even our righteousness includes shades of ambiguity and sin, and often the offense has two or more sides.
- Focus on feelings first. Restrict the participants to "I" statements or declarations that take full responsibility for their own emotions and reactions rather than blaming the other.
- Make sure each gets a fair chance to speak and that each feels heard by the other. Require each to paraphrase the other's words empathically to the other's satisfaction before responding with his or her own feelings.
- When both or all feel heard, a more focused problem-solving phase can begin. Direct the parties to focus on specific and concrete behavior that has been offensive. Make sure the offended person is specific about the behavioral change he or she requests.
- Block efforts to force or demand an internal repentance or change of heart. Such a change is possible, but such a demand may set up a paradoxical bind (since feelings cannot be dictated) that prevents any agreement about behavioral change.

Stuck Structure: Confused Levels

The step-by-step process Jesus gave us for confronting an offense, when supplemented with mid-level strategies such as the group conference and conflict resolution sessions, illustrates the principle of attempting to solve problems at the right systemic and logical level so as not to create a bigger problem. The process ensures that enough people but no more than necessary are involved.

In many cases, we need to discern the level of the problem so that we can respond to it at the right level and avoid creating a bigger problem. Knowing that we create bigger problems by addressing issues at the wrong level emphasizes the importance of taking time and effort to identify the right level.

Often for a congregation to get unstuck, its leaders need to see how its formal structure and informal emotional system create an environment for problem formation. Often aspects of the formal and informal levels are in conflict, sending contradictory messages and undermining each other. We need to play something like the role of a chiropractor, seeing beneath the symptoms to the rigidity, misalignment, inadequacy, or confusion of structures that block effective communication and function—and then we need to adjust these structures.

What do I mean by the "wrong" level? The level can be "wrong" in that it contradicts a formally or informally agreed-upon function of a different level. For example, the pastor or congregation president, given formal authority for a particular task, finds his authority undermined when members choose to get things done at a different level of the system. Such situations send a confusing double message: "You're in charge—but not really." Or: "You'll be held accountable, but don't expect us to give you the power and authority you need to succeed." When we require a leader to accomplish a task, we must give him or her the power or authority to get it done, if we want the leader to stay sane, healthy, and effective.

Another example: A board is entrusted with decision making for a congregation, but certain board members do not share feelings and information pertinent to decisions while gathered in official meetings. They do their important information sharing outside the meeting in informal cliques and triangles that exclude others and allow secret power tactics. This behavior involves decision making at the wrong level (informal subgroup instead of formal group), a tactic that can result in crazy-making binds, especially for those who are supposed to have the same level of information and power but have had their power undermined by exclusion from the informal process. A pastor who is effective with congregational boards works hard to get them to accept the rule, "If it wasn't said in the gathered meeting, it wasn't said. If it didn't happen here, it didn't happen."

The systemic level at which we try to solve a problem or meet a need can also be wrong in that it lacks the complexity, competence, developmental readiness, or appropriate role in the organization to do what we ask of it. The classic example: asking children, or those in the functional role of children such as novices in the organization, to lead or make executive decisions for the whole system. A variation: A parent or the functional equivalent of a parent—the pastor, an elected chair, an informal matriarch or patriarch of the congregation—skips the peer level and builds a primary coalition with people at the functional level of children in the system (nonleader members of all ages) to impose his or her way on other leaders. This is called a "cross-generational coalition" because it crosses generational or role levels in the system inappropriately, including "children" (nonleaders) where they do not belong and excluding parent figures from where they do belong.

Confusing binds are usually avoided and people feel respected and empowered if we do two things that go together in a somewhat paradoxical way. First, involve and inform all the people who have a right to know and to be involved, and make the most of teamwork to solve problems. Second, involve as few levels as possible and approach each problem at the simplest, least inclusive systemic level possible, with the least force required to solve the problem. When people do not try to solve their problems with each other in the simplest, most direct ways, and instead bring in more people (e.g., through informal political coalitions and emotional triangles), and more authority or power than necessary, the strategy often feels like an act of violence to the one being "corrected."

Over- and underreactions, such as leaping to too high a level or not moving to a higher level when needed, usually grow out of abuses of power or anxiety and anger gone out of control. Such emotional reactiveness needs to be calmed before people can think clearly enough to discern the level at which to address the issue. A limited time-out or waiting period and rational discussion of the levels and options available can help. Emotions need to be expressed. Not only rational talk but also expression of emotion is generally helpful only when expressed at the right level, to the right people, and at the right time and place.

Authority Figures and Offense

When the offender and the offended one are not at the same level in the system—one has more authority or a higher symbolic significance—temptations arise to avoid straightforward dealings. The possibilities for confusion and stuckness are greater than if those involved were at the same systemic levels. One such example is when a member, for good reason or ill, feels offended by the pastor.

When a pastor is perceived as the source of offense, many members see little chance of a fair confrontation because the playing field is not level. Feeling on an unequal footing, people may take their complaints to board members, friends, family members—to anyone who will listen except the pastor. Too often others are eager to listen sympathetically and gossip later. One-sided and covert emotional triangles multiply, complicating the situation. Gossip in triangles starts vicious social feed-back loops that can amplify a small problem into a big one.

Of course, in this day of lawsuits and distrust of authority figures, pastors may feel, sometimes justifiably, that the playing field is tilted unfairly the other way. The pastor never knows how many people have been hooked into the complainant's perspective and emotions, and how much distorted gossip has gotten out. The complaining member may refer to "others" who share the same feelings but refuse to name names. Such complaining can be disturbing and unfair to the pastor: it is emotionally manipulative and vague, and one cannot know how to respond appropriately without the facts.

The pastor may fight dirty by pulling rank intellectually or by flaunting clergy status and authority. Such a conflict is a recipe for disaster, since neither player is likely to fight fair when each perceives the set-up to be unfair. And even if the pastor has offended, everyone must play fair for the health of the system.

Pastors can and should take initiative to create a more level field by meeting members on their own turf, by taking a one-down position in listening, and by openly hearing criticism and apologizing when wrongs are revealed. Other congregational leaders should help pastors create level playing fields by mediating or refereeing confrontations to assure mutual respect and to protect all parties from dirty play. Leaders should also maintain a primary co-leadership alliance with the pastor and refuse to be hooked into emotional triangles or cross-generational coalitions with friends or family whose secret aim is to attack the pastor or control the group.

When each level of communication, development, power, authority, subsystems, and logic is matched and coordinated with the others and our problem-solving efforts address the problem at the right level, we can make much progress solving otherwise stubborn organizational and emotional tangles.

Questions

1. How does your congregation handle anger and conflict? What are the unwritten systemic rules and beliefs about anger and conflict? Are these biblical?

2. Does avoidance of conflict preserve the unity of the church?

3. What role does scapegoating play in your congregation?

4. How can conflict be constructive, even creative, and strengthen your relationships and your congregation's identity and sense of mission?

5. What are the methods your congregation has developed for bringing reconciliation between members? What about confession and reconciliation involving groups and boards or the whole congregation?

6. Does your congregation give members time, space, and support for the grief work involved in forgiveness?

7. How does your congregation restrain those who seek to hold it emotionally hostage?

8. How does your church/congregation/synagogue protect its pastors and other leaders from sick and evil behavior of members and how does it protect members from sick or evil behavior of pastors and leaders?

CHAPTER 7

Mishandled Grief, Shame, and Change

Besides conflict, three other common but powerful difficulties—grief, shame, and change—are frequently mishandled and turned into problems.

Mishandled Grief

Coping with significant loss—of loved ones, well-being, or hopes and dreams—and the resulting grief may be life's greatest difficulty. If pastors single out a difficulty whose mishandling leads to the largest number of emotionally potent problems, this would probably be the one. Mishandled grief can be as dangerous as this descriptive phrase suggests: "heart blockage in the body of Christ." The wisest problem solvers, aware that mishandled grief often underlies or reinforces stuck situations, find a way to get to the heart of the matter for healing and health.

Grief's "Easy" Solutions

Grief is often hidden. People may be unwilling to face and feel the source of deep pain. The easier "solution," at least in the short run, is to put our pain elsewhere—bury it, run from it, displace it, or project it. It is easier to express anger, display a façade of optimism, seek pleasure or material goods, and busy ourselves in ways that shift our focus away from pain. American society, with its time pressures, consumerism, and focus on appearances, makes it difficult to stay in touch with feelings.

Our culture makes it acceptable to develop addictions that keep us from feeling pain. Indeed, this culture's aggressiveness and violent spirit make it seem necessary to armor ourselves with defenses and addictions to cope at all.

However, either we learn to live in the garden of our feelings and provide the nurture they need, or we lose our grounding in the life-giving emotional soil of our souls. Part of this nurture involves finding emotionally safe places to share our pain with others, including fellow members. Either we share our pain, or we inflict it on others or ourselves. Pastors and congregations, if they have noticeable weaknesses in helping people cope with pain or if they do not provide a safe place to express deep pain, make handy targets for angry emotional defense tactics from those hurting deeply.

Stuck and hidden grief is more complicated. People stuck in the grieving process may cling to rage as a way to avoid pain and to express loyalty to lost loved ones or lost hopes. Letting go of the pain and rage feels like letting go of the dream or betraying the departed loved one. Grieving people who attempt to cope with pain by angrily attacking the pastor or a group in the congregation (especially if the attack is masked by apparent good intentions) are not likely to express their grief openly without emotional support in a safe environment.

The two most intense and knotty problems I have encountered in the church were both related to a member's loss of a loved one. It is easy to see now, but the picture was not so clear at the time. In both cases, members were upset with me over issues purportedly unrelated to their grief. After sorting through layers of anger, criticism, and destructive triangling, my gut told me that unhealed grief was keeping the system stuck. But I could not lure the grief out into the open and get a handle on it. I am convinced that if I could have found some way to touch the grief, help the sufferers get unstuck, assist them in finding a different way to express loyalty to the lost one, and let God's healing begin to flow, other parts of the stuck conflict would have been freed.

Pastors and other leaders could hardly make better use of their time and energy than to focus on ministry to people in grief, especially if a broader range of losses is included in this category. A grieving person who has felt deeply understood and cared for can be a source of love and appreciation at the heart of a congregation for years. An enraged member with confused or unhealed grief can triangle in many people, construct powerful double binds, and create a stubborn congregational conflict or a depressing atmosphere that resists efforts to bring healing.

Blocking Grief Creates Paradox

Much of the earlier discussion of paradox applies with special power to dealing with grief. Many of our cultural and religious beliefs about grief put grieving people into pathological paradoxes that compound their grief. This phenomenon stems primarily from our tendency under the old paradigm to try to control what cannot be controlled and to try hardest when chaos seems most threatening. If we mishandle grief in the ways so common in our control-oriented, pain-avoidant society, we create problems.

In addition, common cultural rules about grief are reinforced in congregations with overlays of pious-sounding rules and rationales:

> "Be strong by staying controlled at the funeral."
> "Hold it together."
> "Don't show too much emotion, especially not anger."
> "Give it a few weeks or months, and then get done with it."
> "Don't keep talking about it."
> "Let go of the loved one and get on with life."

These typical rules impose a solution that creates disturbing and binding paradoxes. They create dilemmas in which we must deny important aspects of our humanity and of the nature of healing. They suggest, as usual, that control is the solution and the pious response when, in fact, control obstructs the grief process.

The "no-talk" solution is a particularly tough systemic rule in the case of grief-related emotion. We become charged with anxiety about keeping a lid on such powerful emotions as pain, fear, helplessness, guilt, and rage, and avoiding the shame of revealing these feelings. The "no-talk" rule is also a major obstacle to assessing stuckness: Silence can obscure the fact that unhealed grief has anything to do with the emotional constriction in the atmosphere. Pastors and congregational leaders might explore the possibility that unhealed grief is at work whenever they encounter rigid emotional constriction, especially the inability to let love and joy flow through the atmosphere of the gathered group.

The atmosphere of one medium-size congregation that once flowed with energy and openness had come to feel stiff and closed. A new pastor assumed, as call committee members had said, that his strong sense of vision and energy would energize the congregation. But after several years of such efforts the atmosphere was even worse. He finally realized that his approach was not working and decided, on the advice of a wise longtime member whom official leaders had ignored, to explore what had occurred when a previous pastor was forced to resign. He found deep wounds of offense and grief to which he could minister. Secrets came to light. The congregation began to discuss the past openly. People and relationships began to heal, and energy and openness returned.

To work through grief and to heal, a full range of emotions must be expressed and heard. Anger is one of the most important of these. We must face much pain to crystallize grief, cleanse the wound with tears, and honor the depth of meaning of the lost love to ensure that the loss is not trivialized. Hospital chaplain William Miller points out in his book *When Going to Pieces Holds Us Together* that a terrible falling apart is often a sign of strength and is necessary for healing grief.[1] Paradoxically, only then can the lives of those who grieve be knit back together in a new way that integrates the trauma of loss, allows them to finish their primary grief work, and establishes the groundwork for a positive future. Grieving people need both inner strength of identity and a supportive social context to "go to pieces." They need pastors and congregations that understand and bless the pain and chaos of the grief process.

Circular Grieving

Grief is more circular or spiral than linear. The griever does not proceed in a straight line or go through each stage only once. Efforts to force grief into straight lines and boxes can result in a stuck process. Grieving people need to circle back to old painful feelings that break them up. They need to talk again and again about feelings, about the lost loved one and the loss of other parts of themselves (hopes, dreams, reputation, status, financial security, health) that were central to their identity. They need to find ways to carry the loved one within their heart, to express love and loyalty in their ongoing life, to balance the scales of emotional debt for all the lost one has given them. They may need much time to work through their grief and to redefine themselves—months, years, a lifetime. Over time, the pain of grief may ease and be transformed in life-giving ways, but it will never—and should never—totally disappear, because it is part of life's meaning. Some of the pain remains a difficulty with which we must learn to live, not a problem to solve.

More often than not, people get stuck precisely because others try to solve the pain and difficulty of grief with rules based on the idea of making grief go away. Some "nice" religious people discourage others from honestly expressing pain, guilt, shame, fear, helplessness, and rage. These "nice" helpers do not support grievers in going to pieces, nor do they have the empathy, unconditional acceptance, and long-range patience to listen over and over. They don't encourage the expression of ongoing love and loyalty to the lost ones, which would allow a griever to heal and let go of grief's life-stealing aspects.

Honoring Invisible Loyalties

Expressing love and loyalty is an underestimated part of healthy grieving. Many of our cultural instincts, in the United States at least, lead us to cut ourselves off from the past. On the whole, ours is not a culture that exalts the wisdom of the elderly, values the lessons of history, feels much obligation to the past, or sees much connection between past and future. For these reasons, attention to the past and to deceased loved ones, in the sense of honoring them and learning from them, internalizing them and consciously weaving them into our future, presents something quite different from our usual solutions.

A number of family therapists teach that many choices and behaviors are virtually determined by "emotional justice accounting"—a term for the way individuals and emotional systems keep track over the years, often unconsciously, of emotional debts or obligations.[2] This sense of loyalty and emotional justice accounting is largely unconscious and invisible, but it is perhaps more powerful as a result. Many behaviors and choices we observe in families and in the core emotional group of church families involve the exercise of "invisible loyalties" and making the accounts balance with those who have gone before us and to whom we owe much. In fact, we are free to choose in the present only insofar as our choices somehow fulfill our role in the multigenerational emotional accounting of loyalties.

At each critical point, the solution to stuck grief tends to be paradoxical. It is a healing paradox that, as we empathically stand with someone where they are without pushing them to move out of their pain, they are empowered to heal and move. As we accept their anger, they can begin to let it go and to face the pain and fear underneath. As we create a safe environment in which they can go to pieces, they begin to be knit back together. As we encourage them to love, honor, express loyalty, and repay emotional debts to departed loved ones, they are better able to separate from the departed and to develop healthy relationships.

Congregations Grieve Too

These points about grieving apply to members who lose a pastor or friend who played a significant role in the congregation's emotional system. They apply also to the congregation corporately. As organic, systemic entities, groups like families and congregations need to grieve. New pastors often miss this insight. Out of insecurity or misguidance, they criticize predecessors or insist that former pastors be forgotten, ignored, or excluded from the congregation's ongoing life. This mistake makes it more difficult for members to bond with the new pastor as well as to heal their grief at the loss of former pastors.

Helping a congregation grieve as a whole is as crucial for the systemic emotional health of congregations as it is for individuals. Grief is more complicated for congregations. Simply because of logistics, identity is often weaker and more diffuse for large groups. The scope, depth, and rate of change today bring so many losses that, for a large congregation in a mobile area, the issues pile up quickly; time is scarce to grieve and to reconstitute corporate identity. Failure to grieve leads to a cycle of continually weakening congregational identity.

Just as children and people with diffuse identity may have trouble grieving, so will a congregation with diffuse identity. If we do not know who we are, it is difficult to understand what we have lost and what the loss means to our identity. We cannot go to pieces in order to be knit back together if we as a group are already disconnected. How can we grieve together if we have no identifiable corporate "heart," no shared history or boundaries where we can locate the grief and weave its dark strands into a shared tapestry of meaning?

In such cases, good leaders must keep in mind that, as with young children who experience loss, group members may only much later understand what they have lost and what it meant to them. Grief work often needs to be woven into the congregational identity over many years. This work can be done by conducting farewell rituals for departing members or pastors, or by telling stories about the congregation's past at potlucks or special gatherings. This storytelling may include talk about loved individuals now departed and other significant losses as well as joyous events. Storytelling helps remind the members who they are as a congregation and how they have coped with these events by the grace of God.

In many cases, congregations have a clear enough sense of who they are as a people that they can grieve if given the chance. But the absence of systemic thinking about grief often combines with rules not to talk publicly about such things, and members get few chances to speak openly about their loss and their feelings.

An extreme example of group loss is a congregational split or the departure of a whole group of members. Such an event can profoundly threaten a congregation's identity and future. In one small church that had a somewhat reserved style, no one talked in public for years about the loss of a group of beloved members who had split from the congregation. The issues and the loss were too threatening. Entering this congregation at worship was like walking into a funeral. The group was demoralized. Emotion was suppressed. Anger was hidden. New members were rare, and the sense of hope and mission was dwindling. The congregation was unconsciously stuck in grief. Members needed someone who cared to risk breaking the secrecy, help them grieve, and weave this loss into a story that gave hope for the future. Perhaps they needed some public rituals to help them crystallize grief as part of their common history.

Symbols and Rituals

Use of symbolic actions and objects can be particularly helpful in crystal-
lizing corporate grief. We all know the importance of flowers, cards, hot
dishes, or potlucks at the right time. Such symbols not only surround a
grieving individual with love; they can also help the whole congregation
share in the grief. In a grieving congregation, a ritual could include hug-
ging one another and then symbolically embracing the congregation by
circling the altar or pulpit and closing in with a group hug.

My congregation walked a trail of tears, confession, and resolution
with American Indians to share in their grief on the quincentennial of
Columbus' voyage to America, the beginning of a tragic era of losses for
Native Americans. No mere words could have accomplished what that
symbolic action did in the face of the overwhelming grief of these Native peoples and the church's complex guilt feelings. Another congregation helped members make the transition in a merger by holding a special ceremony of recognition for those who gave up their building. The
ceremony included putting a special stained-glass window from that
building in an honored place in the larger church's sanctuary.

Use of perishable objects or symbolic actions may be preferable
because they have less potential to petrify into idols we are never allowed to change. Symbols like water, food, air, oil, earth, and fire were
richly used in Scripture and are still used in sacraments and other traditional rituals. People can choose symbols for unhealed griefs and design
a ritual in which the symbols are exchanged, changed, buried, or burned
to symbolize letting go. Some of the best symbols relating to grief have
to do with living, growing objects, such as plants or trees, which com-
bine permanence, change, and perishability.

One example is given by family therapist/consultant Evan Imber-
Black and family therapy educator Janine Roberts in their book *Rituals
for Our Times: Celebrating, Healing, and Changing Our Relationships*.[3] A couple lost a hoped-for baby in the sixth month of pregnancy.
In the spring, they created a special ritual and planted a flowering plum
tree to symbolize both loss and hope. The mother said, "It puts all the
pain in one place for us." The couple had three other children, but each
spring when the tree bloomed, the couple wept and thought about the
child who might have been. The tree and the act of remembering helped
them not to confuse the lost child with the other children. One spring the

children planted flowers around the tree and surprised their parents by saying, "Now the tree's not alone. They're all connected."

The story illustrates how a symbol and ritual can help us crystallize grief, honor the lost loved one, and prevent the grief from becoming misdirected or mixed up in other relationships. Well-designed rituals might similarly help congregations deal with grief in healthy ways.

Sometimes in handling grief it is best not to experiment too much but to stick with tried-and-true rituals and traditions, because grieving is a fragile time and grieving people may fail to appreciate new rituals. However, on many occasions grief is uncrystallized, unnamed, and stuck; and we need to find creative ways to name it, free it, and give it a chance to heal. On these occasions we go counter to our natural reactions and devise a new kind of cooperative, creative action to get unstuck.

U-turns at Transitions

Losses, crises, and transitions offer opportunities to get unstuck, if we handle them appropriately. In emotional matters, missed opportunities to heal or resolve an issue only rarely are totally lost. Life moves in circles. Even when it is linear in the short term, even when it spirals in one direction, it continues to move in circles. Problems and stuck points recycle or "recapitulate," both for individuals and for congregations. That is to say, many old griefs, frustrations, conflicts, fears, and other unfinished emotional business will come around again. The reminders often reappear at another time of loss or transition. If we try to solve them in the same old way, we stay stuck. They may disappear for a time, but issues recycle, often in new disguises, until the unfinished business is addressed, until we learn to listen to them and to respond in a way that allows healing to run its course.

Many congregations fail to handle grief or conflict in a way that allows them to come to closure. Fortunately, each time symptoms from unresolved grief or conflict surface, another opportunity arises to get our response right. If the congregation and its leaders have become aware of their faulty solutions, they can prepare to respond differently, to make a U-turn the next time the problem crops up.

Some crises, losses, and transitions are predictable. Anniversary

years will come. Pastors will go. New pastors will be called. Beloved
members will die or leave. We will experience failures, fights, disap-
pointments, and losses of dreams. Other events are less predictable.
Congregations may merge. A pastor may be found guilty of a crime or
commit some less tangible abuse of power. Relations between pastor
and members may not work out as hoped. A member may seek to hold
the congregation emotionally hostage, using gossip, financial leverage,
or implied threats of suicide or legal action. Buildings may burn or suc-
cumb to natural disaster. Dealing effectively with unexpected crises may
require us to be ready for an ending and a beginning. Many major opportunities for systemic healing and change occur at significant begin-
nings and endings or at the times of preparation for them.

Whether in the lives of members or in the congregation's corporate
life, few opportunities to free up a stuck emotional system are as powerful and appropriate as ministry to grieving people. We can resolve to
make the most of these opportunities, looking beneath corporate stuck
points to hidden grief. We can receive training in grief ministry through
special programs. By identifying stuck points in the congregation before
big transitions, especially those related to handling grief, leaders can
prepare themselves to guide members along new paths of healing.

Mishandling Change

One of the most difficult challenges the church and synagogue face is
change itself—rapid and often discontinuous, requiring new solutions
and new levels of adaptation. How do we not only learn new solutions
for new kinds of problems but also help congregations come of age and
move to a higher developmental level? How do we help our congregations become what professor and best-selling business author Peter
Senge calls "learning organizations"[4] that can solve higher-order problems by reinventing and restructuring themselves? Radical change demands so much grief work that we cannot keep pace, even with healthy
rules and good skills for handling grief. Overwhelmed, we cling to the
past or, in some cases, dive into change with such a vengeance that we
do not have to feel the pain of loss. Trying to cope by denying and
fighting change or grief may seem to work for a time. In reality, these
strategies create future problems as churches fail to heal and neglect to

learn new coping strategies to defend themselves and to thrive in a transformed world.

We have already discussed the need for members and entire congregations to grieve. The need to adapt to change is somewhat analogous to the need of our bodies to defend themselves against the threat of new diseases. Once-conquered microbes have built up immunity to antibiotics. The AIDS virus is complex, flexible, clever, deceitful, and adaptive. Similar new complexities are evident with emotional and mental disorders.[5] The congregation's defense system must become more flexible, adaptive, clever, and creative and must involve systemic awareness and empowering teamwork to meet these challenges. If we naïvely depend on individualistic thought and old-paradigm strategies like "attack and conquer," "dominate and control," or even "reason it out," we will stand little chance. If we are to become learning churches able to counter the new "viruses," we must use systems thought to help us become familiar with evil's "angel of light" disguises. We need to foster creativity and innovation both in members and in churches as systems.

Our churches need to recreate themselves again and again in ways that honor their history and identity while adapting to the changing mission context. First Church of the Holy Saints had a glorious past. Unfortunately, the more it clung to the way things used to be, the more rigid it became and the less it was able to express the liveliness, dignity, and effectiveness in mission for which it had once been known. In place of its old vibrancy, conflicts continually arose over seemingly petty issues until many members became demoralized or drifted away. To honor the best of its history, Holy Saints needed to adapt and leap to another level of development and to address the changed needs around it.

What do we need to do differently to become learning churches? For starters, we need to (1) foster rules for risk and creativity, (2) honor difference and diversity, and (3) coordinate complexity.

Rules for Risk

Too many churches foster an atmosphere of rules that implicitly discourage imagination, risk, experimentation, playfulness, and second-order learning to move individuals and groups to higher levels of development and problem-solving. The solution to change has been to prevent it or to change only at superficial levels. This reaction is an example of the homeostatic force that protects the balance of systems. But too often an antichange bias has been blessed by our theology as if God too opposed and resisted involvement in profound change.

We can learn from congregations and movements in the broader religious community (such as campus ministry) that reward creativity, risk taking, and innovation in their midst. Lutheran Campus Ministry, of which I am a part, has given yearly awards for creativity in writing, the arts, and leadership (and, at one time, for wearing outrageous clothes at our staff conference!).

One congregation developed a tradition of skits and "roasts" as a way of saying good-bye to departing staff or longtime members. Another congregation arranged tours and dialogue for its leaders with other congregations to compare styles of operation. A congregation could present annual honors to congregational leaders for a variety of services, including awards for the best new idea, the biggest risk, or the funniest event.

Will such innovations meet with resistance? Of course! Efforts to introduce change always run into homeostatic forces. If a church does not have people who informally hit the brakes or slow things down, maybe that role should be formally assigned as a way of making friends with the homeostasis. The church usually does not have trouble finding enough brake-pushers, but we may enhance our sense of teamwork if we bring these individuals into the open and affirm their role, as well as the roles of those who accelerate, steer, shift gears, or find new routes, vehicles, or scenic overlooks.

Honoring Differences

A learning congregation needs also to foster a systemic rule that says, "Different is good." Immune systems and emotional systems tend to mistake the foreign, the different, and the exception as threats and seek to destroy or exclude them. This is an important point, because we deal with so much that is diverse, new, and foreign. In the unique, the exception, the stranger, the different, we find hope for solutions to complex new problems. Indeed, God may be coming to us today precisely in the stranger. The new and the different can play a central part in jolting us out of our ruts, clarifying our identity, broadening our perspective, and stimulating our creativity.

We can encourage openness to the unknown through such strategies as trips to the inner city or to the country or to Central America, or by engaging in ecumenical or interreligious dialogue. First Presbyterian specialized in welcoming the elderly and connecting them with children near its inner-city location. Calvary Lutheran specialized in hospitality and inclusiveness toward less mentally able adults. These congregations' love and vitality seemed multiplied by the encounters.

Even in our Bible studies, we may experience renewal and second-order learning by paying attention to those voices that differ from the dominant traditions. We can explore feminist, black, and Third World theologians and those rediscovering the Hebraic thought forms and methods, such as Midrash, in biblical interpretation.

Coordinating Complexity

If we value creativity and diversity as learning churches, we will increase the specificity of our communication (because those different from us will challenge our assumptions and vagueness), and we will develop leaders with gifts in coordinating complexity. We can also better coordinate complexity if we use instruments such as temperament analyses, family-role learning analyses, spiritual-gifts inventories, and other tools that help us discover, use, and coordinate the gifts of pastors and members. We want to identify particularly good listeners and observers, not only of content but also of emotional processes; people who have the ability to see from a variety of viewpoints, who can think systemically about the chemistry that might result from certain mixes of people and contexts, who can communicate effectively on several levels, and who are flexible and creative enough when they get stuck to make second-order adjustments in problem-solving. Most important is not that we find certain kinds of giftedness but that we pay attention to how gifts fit together and the environment in which they flourish, so that we can put each gift to its best use.

We also need optimal communication to cope with complexity and profound change. We need to include roles for the coordination of complexity in the church so that we can best use all the gifted people God has put in our midst. Valuing creativity, diversity, and complexity and putting them to good use could go a long way toward helping us develop change-ready, learning churches.

Mishandled Shame

Several types of attempted solutions—e.g., scapegoating, secret-keeping, and impression management—involve mishandling the difficult emotion of shame, turning it into a problem. Mishandling of shame is particularly significant in the church because the church claims to have, in the message of God's grace in Jesus Christ, the true solution for shame. Psychologically speaking, shame is a deeper, more powerful, and often more destructive emotion than guilt. Guilt feelings are the painful awareness that comes from falling short of one's own values or ideals. Shame refers to our feeling exposed before others as essentially flawed, inferior, or unworthy to be loved and respected. While we may feel guilty about our behavior, we feel ashamed of ourselves, our identity. The gospel of God's gift of new life in Christ not only forgives our guilt before God, but also gives us, as individual Christians and as a church, a new shame-free identity as Christ's people.

Burden Shifting

When we use scapegoating, secrets, and impression management to handle feelings of shame, we may temporarily disown these feelings (in the case of scapegoating) or cover them up and entice others to think well of us or our group (in the case of secrets and impression management). However, each of these solutions tends to create worse problems down the road. They are what business author Peter Senge refers to as "burden-shifting structures."[6] For example, if a congregation can focus blame and shame on a pastor, member, or group that absorbs the shame and leaves the church (or moves to the inactive fringes), the congregation can feel shame-free for a time, look innocent to itself and to others, and avoid dealing with its own sins and painful issues.

Unfortunately, this apparent solution simply shifts the burden instead of solving it. Scapegoating not only unjustly hurts the scapegoated ones; it also distracts attention from the underlying systemic problem. The congregation is blinded from taking appropriate responsibility and maturing. Adding to the wrongheadedness, the congregation teaches this faulty process to its members, contradicting the heart of the Gospel it proclaims of the One who was scapegoated that all scapegoating might

be exposed and ended. Groups that rely on scapegoating will likely remain stuck in the need to use it if they have not learned any better way
to deal with shame.

Other kinds of cover-up through secrets and impression management also create more problems than they solve. It is true that confidentiality is essential in certain situations and that we need effective interpretation of the congregation's events to the public. Once gossip or a
negative "rap" gets out about an individual or a congregation, it can
complicate a difficulty. But secrecy and efforts to control information
and image are no lasting solution for shame. Once we buy into such solutions, as many in our marketing-oriented society have, we get caught in
a trap of increasing information control and secrecy. This process tends
to become more convoluted and leads to more rigidity in the system.

Choked by Secrets

A shameful secret in a system is like a grain of sand in an oyster. Layer
upon layer is built up around the grain. The resulting pearl enlarges. In
the case of secrets, though, the result is not a thing of beauty. As the
layers build up, the system becomes crowded and choked. Implicit rules
evolve to control behavior and to prevent discussion of certain topics,
lest the feared, shameful secret emerge and spark catastrophe. When
someone touches on a systemic secret, group anxiety shoots through the
roof and the trespasser is greeted by silence, distraction, or scolding.
The offender then realizes that he or she has broken the system's rules.
In an emotional system filled with long-held secrets or a build-up of
rules about what can and cannot be talked about, conversation is like
"walking on eggshells," or the atmosphere is emotionally stuffy. Shameful secrets can be compared to blockages in the respiratory system of the
corporate religious body. They may not cause immediate death, but they
can slowly choke the life out of the congregation.

Secrets as Glue

Secrets may cover up conflict, failures, weaknesses, imperfections, unacceptable feelings, sins, or anything else considered shameful. Sometimes everyone in the congregation—and maybe everyone in the broader

community—already knows the secret but keeps the rule about not mentioning it in public. At other times the secret is known by only a few and functions to cement coalitions—emotional or power triangles in which some draw closer at the expense of excluding others from information and the power that goes with it.

Secrets take many forms and functions. One congregation's secret was the emotional and spiritual abuse many members had suffered from a previous pastor. Another congregation's secret had to do with a pastor's carrying on an affair while his wife was dying of cancer. Still another congregation felt great shame about a conflict in which a group of longtime members left and started their own congregation. I have seen secrets function to help keep a small congregation close while keeping new members out emotionally. I have seen instances in which a senior pastor colluded with lay leaders to keep a secret from an associate pastor to limit the associate's power. When secrets serve as glue, people may not give them up until they learn more respectful and open ways to be close.

"Protective" Secrets and Invisible Dragons

Frequently, secret keeping is declared a necessity to maintain confidentiality or to protect an individual. I have seen situations in which congregational leaders colluded to force a pastor's resignation, without informing the rest of the congregation. The leaders rationalized that secrecy was necessary to protect the dismissed pastor's right to confidentiality. One wonders, in such cases, which leaders and what power arrangements are in fact being protected. Such secrecy may lead to confusion, speculation, distortion of facts, lies, and a closed atmosphere of distrust in the congregation.

Individuals and congregations can deal with difficult situations if they know the truth and have the information they need to make good decisions. When information is withheld, they cannot sort out the truth accurately enough to act confidently, intelligently, and in proportion to the difficulty. They then tend to overreact or underreact and create a bigger problem. Invisible dragons are much more difficult to size up and slay than visible ones.

Openness

Most of the time we are better off knowing more about the dragons, naming them and getting to know them for what they are. Then we can slay them, expose them as fantasy, or take away their fire by making them our friends. We, as pastors and leaders, are usually better off to open up the flow of information in our boards and congregations and "spin" it in a way that is both honest and constructive. Such openness is crucial in an era in which people expect access to information and electronic media have dissolved old boundaries.

The more quickly we name shameful secrets and bring them out into the open, the easier it will be to disarm and slay the dragons or rename them. We can let God's grace shine on the facts and on our faces and call the former secrets forgiven sins or acceptable imperfections. Then we can discuss more openly the appropriate limits on access to information in our churches—limits driven not by shame or by power-seeking but by the team effort to empower our people with the information they need to be faithful members.

Questions

1. What are the unspoken systemic beliefs and rules in your congregation about grief and how it should be handled?

2. How has the grief of individuals, subgroups, and the congregation as a whole been handled in the past?

3. How are loyalties to former pastors and departed congregational leaders recognized and honored?

4. What opportunities or transitions are at hand for your congregation to do a "U-turn" in how it deals with grief?

5. In what ways is yours a learning congregation, or how can it become one?

6. How might emotional or spiritual viruses in your congregational system disguise themselves?

7. How does your congregation bless risk taking and creativity, honor differences, and coordinate complexity?

8. How does your congregation deal with people's anxiety about shame?

9. What kinds of scapegoating have gone on in your congregation, and what issues or shameful sins has the scapegoating obscured?

10. How do secrets in your congregation hold certain people and power groups together and exclude others?

11. How does your congregation, in a context of grace, acknowledge its sins and weaknesses openly to members and outsiders? Or does it engage in impression management and secrets?

CHAPTER 8

The MRI Brief Therapy Skills

So far we have been introduced to the concepts needed to understand systems theory and have seen how core difficulties are often mishandled. In this chapter, we will look at tools from MRI Brief Therapy for dealing with these difficulties.

In the simplest terms, the MRI Brief Therapy Model involves two steps: (1) discerning the attempts at a solution that create or sustain a problem ("the solution is the problem") and (2) intervening to block that solution by displacing it with different, often opposite, behavior ("do something different").

How do we take these steps? Here are several techniques that illustrate the MRI Brief Therapy Model, modified slightly for church leaders. There is no exact sequence in which to use these skills, but they are somewhat sequential: Later techniques build on and depend for success on earlier techniques.

If the groundwork has not been laid, the intervention may have an effect but will likely be unethical, manipulative, weak, or counterproductive. Here are the main skills in more detail.

Skill 1: Connect/Join

Freeing Paradoxes:
* *Give up the illusion of simple communication to communicate.*
* *Meet people where they are to lead them elsewhere.*

Effective pastors and other leaders learn that connecting or joining is the "first base" of all persuasion—indeed, of all significant relational communication. The relationship takes priority over the message. The relationship *is* the message. It is only when we are joined or connected, when others perceive us as fitting or meshing with their inner world, that we can make a significant difference If we have not connected, much of what we think we are telling others and the influence we think we have on systems is shrugged off or misinterpreted.

To discount the need for joining is to remain stuck in superficiality. The patterns and symbols of our emotional worlds need to connect to make a difference. Sometimes this connection happens naturally. At other times it takes an intentional effort. Sometimes we must deliberately build a bridge, walk over it, get to know what the other side is like, and find common ground from experience to bridge our worlds. Call it "joining," "building rapport," "matching," "pacing with," or "creating resonance." The MRI Brief Therapy Model calls it "utilizing client position," and emphasizes that we need to learn the others' assumptions, beliefs, language, images, and frame of reference about themselves and the problem, and use these to help us communicate and persuade effectively.

For example, if a member believes that she cares deeply for her congregation and that her criticism of the pastor helps the congregation, and you take the position that she is evil and uncaring, your message will make no sense to her or will be perceived as an enemy attack. If instead you begin with her frame of reference and agree that she must care deeply to take such a risk and exert such energy, then you may remain in a position to persuade her to show her caring in a different way.

Whatever we call it, connecting is the foundation for the communicating, cooperating, and intervening that get us unstuck.

In my experience, much stuckness between pastors and members begins with failure at this point. When I was a young pastor, most of the mistakes that kept me stuck had to do with not taking this matter seriously enough. I would try to communicate persuasively (often, alas, in the theological language of the seminary) and try to bring change to individuals or systems before I was adequately joined with them—before they were convinced that I understood and appreciated their language and reality adequately, before I was proved to be on their side.

Filtered Hearing

The structure of a relationship serves as a filter for what we hear. It is amazing how lack of joining can distort and block communication. A number of members in one church noted the strong emphasis on the grace of God in their preacher's sermons. But another leader remarked that he never heard any grace in these sermons. How can such a discrepancy be explained? Part could be attributed to communication style and theological differences. More important, however, the pastor had failed to join adequately at the emotional level with the man who never heard any grace. The lay leader felt unloved and judged; he interpreted everything the pastor said through the "filter" of their alienated relationship.

Responsibility to Join

Followers must take some responsibility for joining the leader and letting the leader know how to join with them. It is a two-way street. However, leaders should take primary responsibility and initiative to reveal enough of themselves and learn enough about their followers to make good connections possible from both sides.

No matter how innocent our actions, how right our ideas, how great our talent, or how noble our intentions, we will not be able to lead until we join the team we wish to influence. Serving my first pastorate, I presided at the funeral of the town's former mayor, a onetime member of the congregation. I preached what I thought was a comforting and theologically sound sermon, and I believed that I was caring toward the family. However, I heard later that the family and local citizens were so angry that I was about to be "tarred and feathered and run out of town."

It seems that I had failed to "join" at two critical points. First, I failed to join the community's position of praise for the mayor. I could not agree with those who believed he had earned his way to heaven, but I could have acknowledged their strong feelings about his good life before I appealed to the mercy of God for him. A second matter was brought up bitterly by family members in my follow-up visit: I wore a stocking hat at the graveside service. Never mind that the temperature was close to zero and I did not own a dress hat. This casual stocking hat came to symbolize to the family my total disregard for them and their loved one. All the talking in the world could not patch up the resulting rift. Subsequently, I acquired a dress hat and became more sensitive to the matter of joining.

Can We Join Wrongly?

It is possible to join an emotional system wrongly. A leader can get stuck systemically by going overboard in joining the system and then have nowhere to lead. A congregation may go overboard in joining non-members and forget what it came to offer. One of the best indicators that we have gone too far in joining a system and have gotten stuck emotionally in the system is losing track of our own limits or of the limits and ambiguities in the system, its worldview, and its favorite solutions.

Sometimes newcomers, anxious to prove that they belong, become fanatical about their new group in an effort to establish their insider status. A triangulation that makes you and me feel closer by agreeing that our group is superior to outsiders is a pseudo-joining. It is not a unity based on true knowing and honoring of the image of God in each other. Take away the outsiders whom we disdain, and the sense of emotional unity soon disappears.

Another type of pseudo-joining especially common for pastors is joining a system as a rescuer. If a pastor accepts a call to a congregation and becomes emotionally hooked as its rescuer, he or she is in trouble from the start. This role is generally a hook into a systemic game that pegs people as either victims who need rescuing, persecutors attacking them, or rescuers. The roles can quickly shift if the pastor disappoints expectations.[1] Join the congregation, but do not buy into this pseudo-solution that you can rescue it by yourself, or you will get as stuck as the rest of the system.

Many Ways to Join

How do we join? I find these to be the most useful techniques of joining:

- Listening with empathy, demonstrating accurate understanding and "feeling with," especially in regard to pain and dilemmas.

- Matching or mirroring body language, pacing, metaphors, language patterns, type of humor, and temperamental style.
- Bridging common experiences through self-disclosure.
- Affirmation, confirmation, validation, and respect.
- Using whatever resources the client brings to the relationship (including resistance), by speaking his or her language of words and images, building on strengths, and positively reframing and channeling what might appear as weaknesses.

Effective leadership requires joining not only individuals but also family systems, congregational systems, and larger cultural groups. Joining has a great deal to do with the connections or couplings we make with the system as a whole and with the larger regional, socioeconomic, and national culture of which it is a part. Pastors or leaders who move into a new region or subculture can become diligent amateur anthropologists to learn the subtle assumptions, language idioms, and cherished customs of the area, as well as of the congregation, to join effectively.

Learning to use regional words and phrases and partaking of ethnic food or customs are obvious examples of how to join a culture. But joining symbolically at the level of values may be more significant. In one community I had to learn to downplay my formal education and credentials and to be seen doing practical, physical labor before I became well joined. The regional culture frowned on "tooting your own horn" and tended to value physical labor over intellectual pursuits.

We can join a system by joining with people who play important symbolic roles, such as the congregation's symbolic mothers and fathers. The book *Church Conflict: The Hidden Systems Behind the Fights*, by seminary professor Charles Cosgrove and family therapist/pastor Dennis Hatfield, provides a helpful explanation of joining and mapping.[2] Mapping the roles and relationships in a congregation, as a structural family therapist might do, helps the leader determine how to join a congregation at its significant junctures—the alliances between members, symbolic gatekeepers, memory keepers, and mentoring grandparents. In many smaller congregations, once you have been admitted by a certain key person or group, you are "in" with the whole congregation.

We can also join through rituals. Participating in rituals that are unique to a particular congregation's practice, such as kneeling at a certain point in the service or singing a particular song at the end of worship, can be important to joining. Other informal rituals may be identified and acted out or developed to symbolize joining. Working together every summer on a Habitat for Humanity house, taking an annual canoe trip with the men's group, or assuming a special role in serving an annual dinner can become a yearly ritual that assists joining. Staying for Sunday morning coffee or playing on the church softball team can be a weekly ritual. Birthday parties, baptismal commemorations, cards sent on anniversaries of significant losses—the only limits to the rituals we can use to enhance our joining are time, energy, interest, and imagination.

One pastor cultivated rituals of celebration to help him join with people in failures and painful events. He would bring wonderful homemade bread and wine and throw a party. Either by words, or by actions alone, he would proclaim the grace of God that holds us despite our failures. The pastor embodied that grace through this creative ritual while reframing and changing the meaning of the event with God's cross-embracing, cross-transforming grace.

Honoring Group History and Spirit

Finally, joining a system involves developing a deeper understanding and appreciation of the congregation's story and its strengths, respecting its homeostatic forces (which slow and balance systemic change), and "honoring" its personality and spirit. Heart and spirit are difficult to define in analytical terms, but it is not so difficult to identify the times when the spirit or heart has been wounded, grieved, quenched, twisted, or broken by, for example, abusive leadership. Leaders can profoundly wound group spirit. They can also be gentle emotional stewards, agents of profound healing of group spirit, if they relate lovingly to the gathered group and treat it with respect. When a leader discerns a congregation's heart and spirit and cherishes it, when a leader appreciates the history of God's work in a gathered people and sees, however dimly, God's or Christ's image, individual members often feel the love overflowing to them from the pastor/congregation relationship.

Neither individuals nor emotional systems are inclined to let a leader into their hearts until they are persuaded that the leader will handle their hearts with tender and solicitous care and understanding. Joining a congregation at this level of spirit sometimes takes place only when the leader has shared in individual and corporate suffering or crises and has passed the test of reliability and gentleness. Pastors ought to look at such crises and tests as opportunities to come into their own as leaders.

God Already There

Two friends told me how a visit to Nicaragua several years ago changed their lives. They said, "We went to bring God to the people. We found God was already there more richly than we could have imagined. They ministered God's love to us." Would that more pastors and church leaders displayed such an outlook as they serve their churches! Effective and appropriate joining builds on the doctrine of the good creation and the belief that we are created in God's image (as well as on an awareness of and graciousness toward human beings as sinners). For Christian leaders, it also builds on the belief that the church is Christ's body, that Christians are united to Christ, and that the Holy Spirit is at work in both, making them more Christlike. These doctrines imply that our members and congregations bring resources far beyond what we can see and know. Our role in problem-solving leadership is largely to elicit people's gifts and resources and to release the creative, renewing processes of God already at work in them. This outlook makes it far more likely that we will be able to join effectively and respectfully rather than coming in as supposed rescue experts.

Regardless of the language we use, neither therapy nor church leadership will succeed unless we are joined. And although this process is mutual, the primary responsibility in joining lies with the leader. When things get stuck, the first questions to ask are, "Am I joined sufficiently?" and "Am I wrongly joined and hooked into the emotional system?"

Skill 2: Mark Limits and Responsibility

Paradoxes: Attempting less accomplishes more. One has more power when it is shared.

Early in therapy I like to talk about expectations and try to establish a contract that describes limits and responsibilities. I want to be clear from the start that I hope only to help get the person unstuck and not to try to solve all his problems or change his personality. It is a general rule in brief therapy—and, I believe, the same applies in solving church problems—not to try to solve a problem completely, lest one's utopian goals put the process in an "all or none" framework, create binds that prevent solving anything, and place the therapist or pastor in a rescuer role that fails to increase self-confidence in clients or members about their own resources.

Instead, aim to lessen a problem or improve the situation in small but significant ways. Negotiate boundaries and limits to the problem and your role in its solution. Shrink goals to bite size. Seek large systemic change, if necessary, through small steps. Break a complex problem into smaller pieces. The first step in a long journey is often the most significant and the most difficult. Each tiny spark fanned may become a flame. Use each small step taken and each small goal achieved to build enthusiasm, hope, and momentum.

I also establish boundaries and rules early in therapy that empower me to lead and the clients to stop me openly at any point if they feel disrespected or uncomfortable with the process. I want to establish mutuality in the relationship and the work we undertake while also making clear that I take the responsibility to lead. We create the therapeutic process jointly in such a way that they will be empowered. I will not do everything for them. We will work together to create a solution under my direction.

I believe effective congregational leadership requires much the same approach from the start of a pastor's or leader's tenure and in a congregation's efforts to solve a problem. Expectations and limits of the leader's role should be clear. No leader should accept an explicit or implicit contract to be the rescuer who can solve everything. Co-leaders and followers should be encouraged to stop the leader and draw a line whenever they feel disrespected or uncomfortable. Whenever these people are empowered to participate in defining the relationship and to play a part in creating their working reality, the situation is likely to be life-giving and adaptable and to help them stay unstuck.

The newly developing profession of interim ministry helps congregations get unstuck between longer-term pastorates. I have learned much from skilled interim pastors that reinforces what I have learned from family therapy about achieving healthy partnerships. One of the skills interim pastors commonly use is a process of drawing up a contract for rules of the relationship—roles, expectations, boundaries, goals, priorities, and focus areas. Clear limits and lines of cooperation are established by stating them in the contract. Provision is made for the contract to be adjusted as the congregation's needs change or are more clearly identified.

Besides contracting about the rules of the relationship, skillful interim pastors usually bring new rules (widely accepted in their craft), which allow pain and problems to be named and systemic secrets to be brought into the open so that congregations can be healed and freed from the spell of unnamed pain and shameful fear. These skills of interim pastors—making a contract for the rules of the relationship and establishing healthy new rules, along with a sense of sequential development that breaks progress into smaller steps and accepts a limited transitional leadership role—are similar to the brief therapy skills I describe. These skills may be used by pastors and church leaders in many situations.

Skill 3: Avoid Power Struggles

Paradoxes: Power comes through gentleness ("meekness"). Go "one down" for equality.

Power struggles often rob us of power. They undermine cooperation, paint us into corners, make our positions rigid, and limit our maneuverability as leaders. It is easy to get stuck in power struggles. One example: Two leaders compete for control of a committee but are fairly equal in power and undermine each other so that the committee gets nothing done and both leaders are driven to extreme positions in reaction to each other.

A power struggle can also get stuck when one party in the struggle is a pastor with an official power advantage. Power struggles between unequals, without referees or rules to create a level playing field, lead to more power struggles. In such situations those who feel at a disadvantage often go underground and use emotional guerrilla tactics to narrow the odds. Consequently, the conflict cannot be aired openly, worked out, and finished. If we as pastors, counselors, and leaders wish to foster cooperation and help get a situation unstuck in a relatively short time span, we would be wise to avoid power struggles.

Contract Rules and Consequences

One aspect of avoiding power struggles is to state and agree in advance to clear rules and consequences for breaking the rules. This step may take place at the contracting stages of a call process, a counseling session, or a conflict resolution session, or when a board or group gathers to begin work on an issue. Usually, if no big power struggle is under way, it is best that the leaders guide a group process to negotiate rules. Sometimes, especially at a gathering to work through conflict or in a polarized situation when people are apt to get stuck in a struggle over the rules, a congregational leader can better lay out these rules with a minimum of negotiation and simply ask everyone to agree to them as their ticket to participate. The rules might include such items as "No attacking or blaming," "No dirty fighting," "No monopolizing," "Take ownership of your own feelings and make 'I' statements," "Paraphrase and make sure the other person feels you've heard them before you make your point"—or the leader will call the participant to account and certain privileges may then be denied. Enforcing the rules should not be a struggle between the leader and the rule-breaker but a matter of the leader and the group holding all participants to the agreement.

In therapy situations, it is clear that the therapist is authorized to block behavior that abuses power or breaks agreed-upon rules. Pastors and other congregational leaders often lack such clarity. When there is strong support for this leadership style, counselors and leaders can actively mark boundaries, block problematic behavior, correct faulty communication, lay down new rules, and restructure relationship patterns. Sometimes a pastor or congregational officer can negotiate with the larger group to get support for such directiveness in specific situations. But many people today will not support this kind of leadership from a pastor, even in limited situations.

A fight can be fruitful if destructive behavior is restrained or a respectful solution to differences attained. But when leaders get sucked into a power struggle that cannot be made fruitful, they give up the power of self-controlled leadership, lowering themselves to the emotional immaturity of those to whom they react. In the process, they may "catch" and act out the contagious anger and anxiety that others disown and project onto them. The others avoid facing their own anxiety-creating issues, blame the leader for being angry, and avoid accountability for their reactions.

Go "One Down"

To avoid fruitless fights without relinquishing the leadership role, we can learn a helpful alternative approach from brief therapy. This approach avoids using top-down authority or direct confrontation. The therapist may block a behavior or establish a rule indirectly from a gentle but powerful "one-down position." Our Brief Therapy Model suggests that it is the leader's role to break out of power struggles by giving up attempts both to dominate and to rescue. Instead, the therapist goes with or around resistance, taking a one-down position when power struggles begin.

The counselor backs off, steps down emotionally as if to be lower in power and status, softens tone of voice, or apologizes to or agrees with the counselee. This approach effectively stops an escalating loop and lowers emotional reactivity. The tactic avoids a fruitless fight, increases communication, and leaves the door open for cooperation.

In ministry with college students, it is easy to tap developmentally related rebellion if the pastor tries to be an expert or employs a heavy parental authority. As a campus pastor, no matter how right I am, insisting that I am right or trying to show that I know more than the students about an issue is counterproductive. When I am able to take a one-down position and listen to the ideas and advice of young adults so that they become "experts," I often gain more cooperation and credibility for teaching and leading. Allowing students to be in the "one-up" position of answerers permits me to focus and guide their thinking "from below." Sometimes students ask me for answers and I can speak as an "expert," but it is important to give these answers briefly and then to step back down from the "pulpit."

The flexibility to take a one-down position grows from an understanding that we can reach the same goal by a number of routes. Such flexibility can help leaders preserve self-control under the pressure of attack, calm the attacker, and gain respect and cooperation that enhance the leader's ability to maneuver.

Reframe Resistance Positively

Instead of getting into power struggles with those who resist our leadership, we can understand and use their resistance. We can see others' resistance as their way of letting us know how to work with them and thus as their way of cooperating if we are willing to receive this new information they give us. When a pastor tries to correct a theological error and sparks an angry or defensive reaction, she can push harder and create a bigger reaction. Or she can back off, apologize for being too blunt or for misunderstanding, and then elicit information about the issues behind this doctrinal error and how the issues might be approached more acceptably. Therapists who use MRI Brief Therapy might call this "making a U-turn" to find a different angle of approach.

By making a U-turn to avoid a power struggle, one remains positioned to work cooperatively with several powerful moves. One can gain feedback that helps to modify the approach. Ignoring the resistance, one focuses and builds on areas of cooperation that might otherwise be missed. Resistance can be reframed in positive ways. "Positive reframing" can strengthen the alliance, since one is more likely to be trusted by others if one sees and affirms their positive motives.

Skill 4: Define Solvable Problems

Paradox: The answers we seek may keep us from getting an answer. Big change comes through small change.

Many therapy processes and problem-solving efforts in congregations get stuck because the problem is not defined in a solvable way. If we do not distinguish between problems and difficulties, we will likely get stuck trying to solve insolvable difficulties and undermine our ability to deal with them graciously. Nor does asking why a problem exists and finding someone to blame or returning to a past event that "caused" the problem make it solvable. One "Why?" or blame game tends to lead to another in a circular, escalating fashion. On the other hand, asking "What?" tends to lead to a definition of a solvable problem in a way that suggests specific action. For example:

- "What is happening and what can be done to stop it or change it?"
- "What would we like to be different?"
- "What would a solution look like?"
- "What would a first small step toward a solution be?"

Small, Specific, Behavioral

Frequently, people want a therapist or a congregation to change the way they feel, change the way someone else feels, or change someone's personality. Or they may want to change the church so that it becomes more "spiritual." These are not solvable problems—they are too vague and too big. Feelings, personalities, and spiritual climates may alter as a result of behavioral changes that get a system unstuck. But when we try to change something that can change only spontaneously or by God's working, we create a paradox and a problem. Big, complex, and vague relational problems cannot often be bitten into, let alone swallowed whole without our choking on them. Such efforts are like trying to move a mountain-sized marshmallow by swallowing it all at once. It is important to see how big the marshmallow is so we do not underestimate the task, but we still need to nibble one bite at a time. If we nibble in the right spot, it may eventually topple without our having to eat it all.

Some people say they want to be "happy" or "spiritually fed." But how will we know if the vague goal is reached? We need to focus on specific behaviors, on reachable goals, on how things would look different, and how we would know when a problem was solved or improving.

In one case, a group of members unhappy with the pastor, Carl, created a crisis. Unable to state the problem in a solvable form, the complainants said, "Things aren't good spiritually" and "We can't communicate with him." But they could not describe specifically how things should be different. They wanted to feel good, experience spiritual growth, and communicate well.

These sound like worthy goals. But these vague terms left the congregation confused and frustrated and at the mercy of the complaining group to announce when spirituality, communication, and feelings had arrived at the point of "good enough." There was no way to determine when a solution had been reached or good-faith steps had been taken. The complainants had already decided that no change in Carl's behavior was enough. In their minds, he had been discredited, but they were not willing to admit that their minds were closed. The vagueness and cover-up of their motives meant that no one else had the information needed to help solve the problem, and they remained in control. They had kidnapped the crew and hijacked the ship, so to speak, and were in a position to define the terms of the ransom.

This was not a realistic climate for emotional problem solving because when complaints that sound sincere and innocent are vague, the agendas of revenge, domination, and control can be hidden behind these terms and carried out under their guise. Few people want to see themselves as bitter or controlling, so complainants may even deceive themselves about their own motives.

An outside mediator was brought in, but after a few unsuccessful attempts to pin down the complaints to negotiable issues, the mediator allowed the same vagueness to rule. The complainants were never fully challenged, by the mediator or by church officers, to take responsibility for their bitterness and controlling behavior. The emotional hijacking continued, and no satisfying solution was reached.

Proponents of brief family therapy faced with this situation might use such terms as "communication breakdown" and "not feeling right" so that people would feel that their position had been taken seriously. But the therapist would reframe these terms or build on them to define a solvable problem or to change the situation directly by redefining it. The therapist would ask how things would be different, what the critics would see, how they would know a change had begun, and what small behavioral changes would signify good-faith action and progress toward a solution. Such clarity comes from the leader's skill and use of power, but it results in empowerment of all while preserving the leader's ability to lead.

In cases like the one above, an empowering sense of movement might have emerged if the critics had been pressed to be specific: "We would be happy if Pastor Carl showed he was taking us seriously by varying his style of preaching from week to week." Then Carl could have said, "I am willing to vary my style if you notice and encourage

me in the effort and continue to give me specific information after each
sermon on how I can better preach to your needs." Or the situation could
have been energized if the pastor and critics agreed, "We will know
things are improving if each of us is able to go talk to Pastor Carl and he
listens without putting down or disqualifying what we say for one whole
discussion." Such steps are small enough to be realistic. They can be
verified, taken as encouraging signs, and built on with more steps. Life-
giving feedback loops can be set in place that may lead to better feelings and a larger positive change in the system.

Skills 5 and 6: Identify the Minefield, Discern What Is Different

Paradoxes: Faster is often slower. Go back to go ahead.

These two closely related skills were discussed in earlier chapters. Let
me reiterate that it is a foolish waste of time and a source of unnecessary
risk to set out across a minefield in haste. It is seductive to think that we
will reach a solution faster and prove ourselves noble if we are wounded
in the process. It is much wiser, safer, and more efficient to discern the
failed attempts at a solution and avoid them.

Ask questions about what has been tried, and observe what is being
tried now. The fact that someone says, "I tried to talk to the pastor,"
does not mean that he actually asked to speak to the pastor, explained
the purpose of the talk, and spoke clearly and directly in private with
patience, timing, respect, and willingness to listen. One needs to know
the specifics and to discern patterns such as controlling or avoidance to
figure out what efforts at a solution were attempted and failed. At least
you will then be able to negotiate the minefield of faulty solutions and
avoid making the problem worse.

Most likely, you will also be better able to figure out what doing
something different might mean—perhaps an action that expresses an
opposite pattern of solution. For example, it is not usually effective to
ask someone to stop thinking about an unpleasant experience or to stop
an irritating behavior, because these behaviors are often not under conscious control. It is more effective to ask the person to think about a

pleasant or successful experience or to repeat a positive behavior, and reinforce them when they do.

If we are trying to get someone to stop criticizing the pastor, we can, rather than simply demanding a stop to the criticism, ask the critic to put the evaluation into a certain form. That form might require five affirmations for every negative, and require that the negatives state specific requests for change with a rationale and an explanation of how the person will support the pastor in making these changes. The different behavior in these examples involves not only a pattern change for the critic but also for those reacting to the critic.

Skills 7: Reframe and Utilize

Paradoxes: Shake up certainties to build new confidence. Use whatever they bring to bring change.

"Reframe" means to put a different frame around the picture of a situation so that it takes on a new meaning. "Utilization" is the term for taking the position and resources people bring to us and using them as a lever for change instead of trying to impose our views or wishes on them.

These techniques express a style of working with people based on a philosophy laid out in this book: The more we grasp the systemic complexity and paradoxical nature of life, the more we are able to use what others bring to a relationship (utilization) and put it into a new context (reframing) that allows the situation to get unstuck. There are positive aspects, such as loving and constructive elements, even when someone creates a problem. We will be able to see more clearly the positive side of resistance to change. We will also be able to see better the destructive and selfish aspect of actions that appear loving or unselfish. We will be able to see behavior from numerous perspectives and frame it within a variety of systemic contexts. We will have the flexibility to weave observed facts into a variety of interpretations, each fitting the facts together equally well and making equal sense.

Thus we will be able to choose the story most likely to be useful in bringing about a solution. We will be better able to "sell" a counterintuitive intervention that is most likely to reverse a solution that has become a problem. We will be able to use the strands brought to us to weave a life-giving story.

Reframing is perhaps the most pervasive and useful of the techniques recommended here. Reframing shakes up certainties that keep us stuck by offering a more persuasive interpretation. When we reframe, we have the same pieces of reality. But we put the pieces together in a more constructive and convincing way. We put a different frame around the situation, changing its meaning. Most of the time in pastoral work, effective reframing is all that is needed to make "the difference that makes a difference" and get things unstuck. It is also the least invasive and most efficient kind of helping.

Reframing often highlights exceptions to our view that show us new options. When people are stuck in a problem, they typically interpret it in absolute terms. They also speak with absolute certainty and total resolution about their conclusions. Reframing picks up on exceptions and alternative explanations that cast doubt upon certainties and introduce shades of gray and colors into a black-and-white picture. For example, we may be totally convinced of the insensitivity and hardness of heart in our pastor until someone points out and brings forth evidence that these apparent qualities are a front he uses to disguise the fact that he is easily hurt and afraid to let people know how vulnerable he is, lest they hurt him more.

Much good theology also challenges our theories about people. It increases ambiguity, uncertainty, and awareness of our limits in a way that is humbling, humanizing, and liberating when we have faith in God. Theologically responsible individuals not only can feel comfortable with reframing; they often have a knack for it and reframe with more depth than the typical therapist.

"Utilization" is an attitude central to building cooperation. It is, in a sense, a form of reframing. It refers to creating new solutions with people out of the materials they bring to the relationship, including strengths and weaknesses, cooperative and resistant attitudes. "Utilization" does not look at anything the other brings as waste or enemy. Brief therapy often uses the symptom or problem itself as a doorway or resource toward helping the client. This concept also makes sense in other kinds of relationships. I am reminded of a seminary teacher who specialized in making sculptures out of junk. He chose a wasted furnace room for his office and taught us to pick up whatever we found around us and build our lesson around it.

This whole notion is exemplified by one of the heroes of Strategic and Brief family therapy, hypnotherapist Milton Erickson. While Erickson had no trouble assuming authority and leadership or using hypnosis with extraordinary technical skill, he had a radical sense of respect for his clients. He used what they brought to therapy and rechanneled it to get the clients unstuck so they could solve their own problems. He believed people possessed the strengths and resources to bring about solutions, if they could only be helped to gain access to them. Therapy, for him, was not a matter of giving people something they did not have so much as eliciting their conscious and unconscious resources to bring a solution. I believe pastors and church leaders ought to use what is brought to them in the process of leading instead of trying to impose their way on others. This approach can be especially important in stuck systems.

Skill 8: Use Paradoxical Interventions

Paradoxes: Paradox counters paradox. If the solution is the problem, then the problem is the solution.

We have already touched on many paradoxical interventions. The approach I commend is permeated with therapeutic paradoxes, just as human problems of stuckness are riddled with destructive paradoxes. Counselors conducting brief therapy often design and assign directives or explanations to put clients into counterparadoxical situations that can break them out of a trap. These sorts of "paradoxical injunctions" or "paradoxical prescriptions" can sometimes be used effectively in stubbornly stuck situations in the church as well, especially if we understand that destructive emotional paradoxes can serve as traps that need to be sprung by counterparadoxes.

Some Initial Warnings

Paradoxical injunctions must be used at the right time and in the right spirit, or they are cheapened and lose their power. For example, Helen continually complained to other members that the junior-high Sunday school class she taught was rude to her. John was becoming annoyed with her complaints. He knew a little about paradoxical techniques, so he thought he would try one on her. "Helen," he said, "those kids are rude, and you are failing to do what you need to do as a teacher because you want to complain so you will get attention." Helen got angry and decided to prove John wrong. She stopped complaining. In fact, she stopped talking to John entirely. However, she still had trouble with the class, failed to get the support she needed, and decided to quit teaching.

John's paradoxical approach did something. But its disrespectful tone and poor timing made it more a selfish manipulation for John's own relief than a way out of a bind for Helen. John should first have taken the more obvious steps of encouraging Helen, linking her with experienced teachers who could help, and checking out what she had already tried to solve the problem. Even if it were clear that a paradoxical approach could help, he should not have tried such a ploy unless he could approach Helen in a way that respected her dilemmas as she perceived them and helped her out of them.

Counterparadoxical interventions outside an appropriate relational context can be cheapened to a manipulative technique of "reverse psychology." They can also be used unethically if there is no agreement or contract with people who want our help or if the paradox is aimed at binding rather than freeing people by countering a paradox in which they are stuck.

When paradoxical prescriptions or injunctions are given, they are accompanied by a rationale that makes them seem sensible even though they go counter to common sense. For example, when someone is given the prescription to cause the very symptom she wants to solve, the rationale may be: "You need to bring the symptom about so that you can observe the sequence of behaviors leading up to it and any specific trigger events. As we gain more of this information, we may also discover how to disrupt the sequence or be better prepared to deal with it."

The rationale is true enough. But the client need not know about part of the prescription, and it is probably better left unmentioned, lest its effectiveness be undermined. That is, prescribing a symptom changes its context in a way that disrupts the client's attempted solution. The attempted solution is normally avoidance of the feared situation or event. But the more the client tries to prevent it, the more her fear increases and she comes under control of the problem. The more the triggering situation is avoided, the less able she is to cope with the problem when it appears, and the more demoralized and helpless she feels. If she seeks to produce the symptom, this effort disrupts the attempted solution. While in one sense it purports to change nothing, this reversal actually changes everything. The frame and meaning of the problem are changed. It is put in a different context or broken into parts and no longer has total sway.

These skills have implications for helping get churches unstuck. Positively reframing or prescribing a symptom (such as confusion or conflict or grief or criticism or going slow or staying stuck a little longer until we are ready to change) has a way of changing context and meaning so that the very thing we thought was the problem can become, in this new context, the key to unlock our stuckness. For example, a pastor who asks for criticism may rob it of its destructive power. A leader who persuades a congregation to fight openly to work through its hidden but troublesome differences of vision may enable it to overcome paralyzing fear of conflict and open up discussion of a whole new joint vision. If we are controlled by fear and absolutism or perfectionism, we will never dare try such an approach. But if we are directed by faith in a gracious God and a sense of flexibility in the emotional reality we create together, we may find great help in paradoxical strategies.

Note, in summary, what paradoxical interventions do. They are directed not at changing the perceived problem but at changing the level of the attempted solution that sustains and amplifies the problem. If "the solution is the problem," in many cases, "the problem is the solution."

I do not suggest that pastors and church leaders who feel stuck should run out and start trying paradoxical prescriptions right and left. Therapists do this in the context of a specialized situation in which clients have asked for help solving a problem. They design paradoxical prescriptions precisely to fit and to counter the binding paradox that has the client stuck. They design these interventions in the context of an array of skills after simpler interventions fail, and after careful consultation with others on the therapeutic team. They use what works, even something as simple as helping people realize that what they thought was a big problem is a normal part of life, or helping them notice that they have already started to solve the problem without the therapist's help.

Use Paradox on Yourself

Pastors and other church leaders need a sense of how paradoxes can lead to stuckness and how seemingly paradoxical steps can get us unstuck. However, they should use paradoxical prescriptions only in certain cases —for example, on themselves. A recent application of a paradoxical prescription on myself helped to free me from a trap.

I was caught in a dilemma between spending more time in my office and being out making calls and contacts in the community. Since being out seemed to serve more people, I increasingly spent time in the community. As I used more of my time that way, staff and members who wanted me in the office became more anxious. The more intensely I felt their anxiety, the more crowded I felt being around them and the more often I avoided them and the office. This pattern continued and escalated until their anxiety and anger and my distancing resulted in serious alienation. Someone had suggested that I carry a pager when out of the office. At first I felt that its presence would crowd and pressure me all the more. People would call me constantly, and I would never get any space. It finally occurred to me that doing something different, prescribing something that threatened to worsen the problem—namely, the pager —might be worth a try.

The result? The anxiety of staff and the small group of members eased considerably. They called me very little, but knowing they could reach me helped them relax. I then felt less pressured by them and more comfortable being in the office. A better balance of closeness and distance was achieved.

Paradox in Pastoral Care and Witnessing

Paradoxical prescriptions can also be appropriate in situations of pastoral care, counseling, spiritual direction, and witnessing. A young man once came to me asking for help in his spiritual quest. He had expressed his spiritual desire to friends, and they had pressured him to give his life totally to God. But he did not feel able to give his whole self. Instead, he felt stuck and frustrated spiritually. He asked me for suggestions. In the course of our conversation, I also learned that he had been baptized as a child. Here is the paradoxical prescription I gave him:

- Your friends are right in a way. Faith in God is a response of the whole self. Sometimes faith comes suddenly in a conversion experience. But more often it comes after a longer process in which God has worked to bring a believer to this point. That God has been working in your life is evident from your present desire for faith.
- You are baptized. Do you know what that means? God has already given you all you need for salvation—forgiveness of sin; the Holy Spirit; joining with Christ and the church; a new birth, calling, and identity as a Christian; God's promise to continue working in you to produce faith.
- I suggest that you keep doing what you are doing, going to worship, and reading Scripture.
- Don't try to give God your whole self. Give God only what you honestly can.
- Don't rush it. Take your time. It takes time for faith to grow. Don't make a commitment just because people are pressuring you. Wait to make a full commitment until you are ready. That time may come, as a time comes to make vows in marriage; but give faith time to mature.
- Keep me in touch with your faith journey. I'll see you in a few weeks.

The net result of this paradoxical "go slow" injunction appeared to be a deepening of peace and a mellower but stronger desire to trust God without demanding a big religious experience. The young man seemed to hear the message of God's grace in a way he had not before; he appeared to have broken out of the binding paradox.

Paradox to Free the Pastor

Paradoxical prescriptions may be used effectively by congregational leaders toward their pastors. For example, in some cases clear directives to pastors to work less, to take days off, to take sabbaticals, and to take care of themselves by doing enjoyable things have helped free them from binds. Many pastors feel they must always do more or that others are demanding more of them. This feeling is not always a fantasy. Whether real or imagined, the perception of never having done enough binds

and stresses some pastors to the point of counterproductivity. The harder
the pastor tries to meet demands, the less loving and the more burned
out he or she becomes. Telling the pastor not to feel this way is likely
only to pile up more guilt. In contrast, prescriptions from the congregation's board or lay decision-makers to do less (provided such words are
backed up with supportive measures such as days off, helpers, and commitment to "selling" the prescription to the congregation) may free up
the pastor.

Sometimes board members have to counter their own perception
that the pastor is not doing enough and that the solution is to pressure
him or her to do more. They must see beyond this superficial commonsense solution to the underlying paradoxical trap. Then they can see why
a paradoxical prescription such as "Do less (in a more focused way)" or
"Take care of yourself first rather than others" is the way to bring out
the best in their pastors.

Closure and the Open Door

Frequently at the end of therapy, the therapist using this model will use
one or two paradoxical interventions to prevent destructive relapse into
stuckness. These include the injunction to "go slow" in making changes
and the prediction or prescription of a relapse. The therapist may explain that going slower is healthy because it allows time to adjust and
prevents one from feeling pushed to change faster than one is able. Going slow gives us the chance to test and modify changes so that they will
be lasting.

Relapses may be anticipated as necessary so that people can be
reminded of their previous condition and test whether they really want
the change. Relapses can also help us gain the ability to bounce back
and have more control. Such explanations are paradoxical, but they are
not tricks or deceptions. They are practical and freeing; they make clear
that relapses are normal and that difficulties are bound to continue after
therapy. Relapses or recurrences of a difficulty can never again be seen
in quite the same light; no longer will they be seen as shameful events
that should be feared and prevented at all costs.

The therapist also offers an open-door policy, if former clients
should get stuck again. Return visits to the therapist may be likened to

going to a medical doctor one or a few times to get through a stuck point and then getting on with self-healing until the need arises again. Often, just knowing that such a resource is available makes problems seem less threatening.

If we want change in the church or synagogue to be healthy and lasting, we would do well to follow similar principles both in the process of seeking change and in our approach after a systemic change is accomplished. We ought to go slow, expect and make the most of relapses, and maintain a relationship with someone equipped to help us get unstuck again if needed.

Using Creative Rituals

I have discussed how difficult it may be to address a whole system. Rituals provide such access to systemic wholes, and people will often accept new rituals or new uses of old rituals in a religious setting. Congregations or boards can be helped in getting unstuck if we can design creative rituals, or rituals that "hit the spot."

We can ask ourselves what kinds of rituals are already in place, including informal and unrecognized ones, such as an argument that sounds like a broken record or people doing the same old things again and again. Are these rituals helping keep us stuck or unstuck?

One congregation's board experienced hard feelings over a misunderstanding. Board members had talked things out as best they could, but they seemed unable to clear the air completely. They decided to use a ritual the pastor had taught them in which a large bowl of water and a towel were placed on the table in their midst. Each person was invited to have his or her hands washed by another and then to wash the hands of whoever came next to be washed. In the process, members washed and were washed by others with whom they had been at odds. Even though there had been reconciliation, this ritual seemed finally to bring closure in a way words alone could not.

Rituals can also help resolve conflict. For example, what if two associate pastors are locked in a disagreement they cannot resolve? The staff committee might assign an "odd days and even days" ritual. On odd days one associate's point of view on a given issue is to prevail without argument and the other associate is to listen and observe to learn

as much as possible. On even days the roles are reversed. On Sundays
the two spend some time talking over what happened.

Rituals can make confrontation both more humane and more powerful than a direct verbal approach. Imagine a board whose members keep
passing responsibility or blaming others. What if they were to start a
ritual in which any member who observes "buck-passing" takes out a
dollar bill and silently begins passing it around the group? The dollar
keeps going until someone takes responsibility to tackle the problem at
hand. Whoever admits to "passing the buck" or decides to take responsibility to make a difference gets to keep the dollar.

Visualize a situation in which one person or group has an annoying
way of dominating every discussion while others support this behavior
by staying silent. A simple ritual might be designed to make sure every
person takes a turn speaking at each meeting, to ensure that each time one
side of an issue is represented, the other side is also heard. At the campus
ministry I serve, a ritual at our weekly luncheon consists of each stu-
dent's telling the "high point and low point" of the week. As simple as
this ritual is, it has been popular and powerful in helping each person participate, in giving us a sense of continuity, and in deepening relationships.

Sometimes a pastor, board of directors, or committee can design a
ritual that has a counterparadoxical flavor or that effectively reframes a
situation.That method typically discerns the unhealthy, unproductive
way events usually proceed and then prescribes them with some modification. As in family therapy, symptoms might be scheduled to occur in a
precise, alternating pattern, or people might be assigned to play out their
usual roles in precise, symbolic ways. If certain members of a board
seem stuck in criticizing, either outside the meeting or at a point in the
meeting that demoralizes or controls the process with bubble-bursting
aplomb, the "critic" role might be ritualized. The council could sched-
ule time during a meeting to hear criticisms within certain well-defined
parameters, perhaps followed by someone assigned the role of making
affirmations.

Dysfunctional rules and rituals, paradoxically, are changed when
they are prescribed. They are changed further when they are prescribed
with modifications. They are put in a different context and may take on
different meaning. Criticizing is not the same when one is being asked
to do it within the group meeting instead of in secret before or after, and
in a way that does not control the decision-making process.

We need rituals. If we do not have enough adequate, life-enhancing rituals in our churches and groups, the informal and unacknowledged rituals that evolve to fill the vacuum may do more to keep us stuck than to free and humanize us. Rituals help keep us stuck when they become absolutized or petrified and coated with implicit "no change" rules. Rituals may also keep us stuck by becoming so rigidly linear that the rich symbolic and emotional possibilities are squeezed out.

Although I have suggested the use of rituals for more than worship, the corporate worship gathering is one place where we can observe the constricting of rituals in many congregations. We can learn some helpful differences if we contrast the frequent "hardening of the ritual arteries" in many white congregations to the rituals of young people at rock concerts or to worship at many black congregations and churches in the developing world. These more "circular" styles of worship ritual often reach out and draw people in, involve more shared leadership roles, tap many emotions (as well as the mind, body, and senses), build in dramatic and narrative movement, and use a rich variety of symbols.

I will never forget the first time I attended a certain African-American Methodist congregation in Memphis. All of these elements were present. Numerous members came out to the parking lot, welcomed people as they got out of their cars, and walked the newcomers inside to make sure they were well situated. As the service continued, it was as if the congregation's story and that of the people and their neighborhood were knit together and woven into the biblical story.

Rituals are even more the church's and synagogue's stock-in-trade than the systemic therapist's. We do not have to remain ritual-starved or analyze, "relate," and "talk to death" everything we do to get unstuck. Some truths are better expressed in ritual. Neither need we get stuck in linear rituals rigidly performed without flaw, fuzziness, or "play in the line." Keep in mind the circular, inclusive, and life-enhancing purposes of ritual for relating, changing, healing, expressing beliefs, and celebrating. We live by grace with a God whose nature is creative, redeeming love, ever new, yet ever constant. Why not tap our creativity by planning and using rituals to help us get unstuck and stay unstuck?

Questions

1. How well are your leaders "joined" with the congregation and its key subgroups emotionally? Does the connection involve emotional rescuing or teamwork?

2. Are limits and expectations of the leaders' roles clear? Can the relationship between leaders and followers be openly discussed and renegotiated when either is feeling uncomfortable?

3. What hidden or open power struggles are going on in your congregation? Are they helping or hindering your congregation's emotional balance and mission? Who needs to take a one-down position to get things unstuck?

4. How might you break your congregation's big problems into bite-size, solvable ones whose solution would build morale and momentum?

5. Are problems defined in specific, behavioral, solvable form in your congregation? Or are complaints vague, past-oriented, or blaming?

6. What attempts at solution have been tried and failed? What approach would be 180 degrees different?

7. How might you reframe the problem in a more life-giving way? How can you take the resources at hand (including what looks negative) and use them to create solutions?

8. What paradoxical prescriptions might help free up your leaders and members? What rituals, formal or informal, in your congregation are freeing and humanizing? What rituals keep you stuck? How do you create new rituals?

CHAPTER 9

Circular Assessment

The words we use to assess situations and define problems matter, but so does the process by which we assess and define. Often a circular assessment process can be a significant part of the solution. "Circular" here points to the web of interrelationships and mutual influences in problem formation and resolution.

Problems defined circularly (by describing what behavior precedes and follows so that we can visualize a sequence of behaviors coming full circle and exerting mutual influence) and addressed by a circular process (involving people and viewpoints surrounding the problem) are often more solvable than problems defined linearly (cause/effect) through a linear process. Circular processes shift the focus from shame and blame for the problem to shared responsibility for a solution, thus minimizing defensiveness and denial. Everyone feels heard and taken seriously.

Holy Foundation Church has lived through numerous conflicts over the years and has a reputation in its community for continual stirrings of dissatisfaction. Yet every time a subgroup tries to confront the congregation's stuckness, it runs into a wall of denial from both formal and informal leaders. Either those complaining get no response and no change, or if they push the point, they are criticized and blamed for any existing problem. Leaders buttress their denial with words like these:

"Our church would be better off if that group went somewhere else."

"Sure, we have a few rough spots. Some people are never satisfied—but just look at all the good things."

The lay leader of another congregation got fed up with complaints and criticisms brought to him about the new pastor. He told complainers they were the problem, and everything would be fine if they stopped complaining. Angry and frustrated, incapable of understanding how to tackle the concerns, he could not hear a legitimate message in the complaints. Complaining members reacted to being blamed by becoming angrier. The lay leader was stuck in his emotional reactions, and the congregation was stuck in a vicious circle based on attempting to handle members' concerns by arguing, criticizing, and silencing.

The lay leader was driven partly by his belief that he was defending and supporting the pastor. But in fact, he was postponing and aggravating the pastor's future problems by his protectiveness. He did not realize that the pastor could be better protected by bringing these complaints to light so that they could be dealt with directly and fairly, even if a bit painfully. Had he not been hooked into an emotionally reactive stance, he could have brought people together, laid down rules for fair and respectful airing of concerns, and played a mediating role in the discussion. The congregation might then have been able to work through to understanding and reconciliation. Even if the outcome was to agree to disagree, this strategy could have broken the impasse and returned the situation to the status of a difficulty rather than a problem.

Field Complaints with Respectful Openness

What could members and leaders have done to be more effective in these situations? The skills of circular process could have made a huge difference. First, pastors and executive leaders should make sure that people with complaints and criticisms receive a fair hearing and that they follow a respectful process. A common form of disrespect is to avoid communicating directly with the person with whom we are upset and instead to work informally through a third person. Leaders who get emotionally triangled with dissatisfied members and treat the pastor as an outsider create the functional equivalent of cross-generational coalitions in families. If such coalitions are not replaced by a primary working alliance and open communication between the pastor and other high-level leaders, little can to done to solve the problem.

On the other hand, leaders who try to solve difficulties by totally squelching complaints about the pastor cede leadership to more negative members. When scorned, negative people go underground in the emotional system, where they use guerrilla tactics and avoid being held accountable for destructive behavior. They turn their anger against official leaders and undermine these leaders' credibility by active or passive resistance. Paradoxically, when leaders, including the pastor, encourage criticisms to be aired openly and directly (perhaps with mediation) to the target of the complaint, the leaders preserve their functional role. They are able to channel anger constructively. They may ease negative feelings, gain respect, build trust, and if they are good at using what is given to them, refocus negative energy in positive directions.

In the process of taking initiative to hear people's feelings such as hurt, anger, frustration, and disappointment, leaders put themselves in a position to discern and define the problem. They can gather more information and have more to work with. They may then learn whether the problem has more to do with the personal lives and emotional issues of the complainers. They may decide that these critics are making mountains out of molehills, projecting personal issues onto the pastor or congregation. People often react disproportionately when a congregational issue parallels a situation in their personal lives. In such cases, leaders can find more appropriate ways to express caring for these members, listening empathically and guiding them to acknowledge their own feelings, or referring them to appropriate support groups or to counseling.

The leaders may also decide that the complaint or concern is not a problem at all, or that it involves difficulties with which we individually or together must learn to cope. Or they may decide there *is* a problem. With more information out in the open, they can define the problem in a solvable way. So long as members' negative feelings are squelched, they are likely to make things worse, and the leaders are unlikely ever to be able to define the problems as solvable. Both in family therapy and in stuck congregations, stating a problem in a solvable form is often the major part of a solution. Bringing complaints out in the open gives us a better chance to define a solvable problem and, if the solution involves people finally feeling heard and becoming reconciled, to solve it in the process.

Accept Feelings, Avoid Triangulation

In many cases, if open, honest discussion and feedback were already taking place in the congregation, discontented members would feel heard, and the size of the problem would be shrunk considerably. Instead, feeling misunderstood and let down by official processes, such members, if they are sufficiently invested emotionally, may turn to informal and underhanded means to get a hearing. Typically, they seek acceptance and empowerment by complaining to others and getting them "triangled" —that is, hooked or "wired"—into their point of view and emotional agenda. People believe they mean well when they turn to triangulation for support. But this ploy creates stubborn, rooted problems. All communication is filtered and distorted through the hidden third person of the triangle. You never know to whom you are really talking.

A second major skill of circular assessment is similar to the Bowen Theory's caution to stay out of emotional triangles. It involves avoiding emotional commitment to simplistic cause-and-effect thinking or to one way of explaining the problem. Using this skill, we gather information and view the problem from various angles to see how people's behaviors are circularly interconnected. Those who can learn the art of hearing and validating feelings on all sides while stating their own views are in a position to start unraveling a tangled problem. Leaders who can perform this task under pressure are worth their weight in gold. Once people feel heard fairly, any remaining problem can usually be defined in a solvable form.

Focus on Self

A third essential skill in circular assessment is to see one's own role in the problem and its solution. This skill is especially important in situations where, no matter what we do, we cannot get our congregation or partners in leadership to face up to a problem's seriousness. Then the primary issue for leaders becomes keeping ourselves healthy and unstuck amid a difficult reality. The more the system is stuck, the more difficult and crucial it is for us to focus on our own feelings and behaviors, because there is more danger of our getting drawn into the emotional quicksand.

Sometimes, paradoxically, it is precisely when we give up trying to fight others' resistance and simply focus on extricating ourselves that real change begins to occur. In Bowen Family Systems Theory much of therapy is oriented precisely to getting people, including the leaders, to quit focusing on others and to zero in on their own emotional issues and on defining themselves—their feelings, beliefs, and vision—to those whom they are leading. This approach may sound selfish, but it is often the beginning of authentic caring and systemic change as it disrupts a feedback loop in which the solution (trying to change the congregation or others) creates a bigger problem (the system's reacting and resisting pressure to change). Church people, especially, need to hear this word, since we so frequently assume that we should focus on the needs of others instead of "selfishly" on ourselves.

Shifting focus back to yourself and working on your own emotional issues is something like achieving healthy detachment in relation to an alcoholic family member, which then prevents you from inadvertently enabling the disease process. Many pastors and church members who focus on taking care of others and getting praise for it feed their own falsely based self-esteem and enable the dependencies of others. The more for which they take responsibility, the less responsibility other members take in a stuck "overfunctioner/underfunctioner" feedback loop. Focusing on self and giving up the effort to change the church to fit your emotional agenda may be just what it takes to break out of stuck feedback loops and solutions that create problems.

Such giving up is related to the key spiritual insights that victory comes through surrender and that God's grace is often most powerful at the point of our weakness and failure. I have noticed in my years as a pastor that when, after running repeatedly into a brick wall, my passion for change in the church is tempered by detachment and surrender, I often have done my best work as a preacher, counselor, and pastoral caregiver.

For example, I used to be frustrated at the poor sermon listening skills of those in the pews. I assessed the problem as a combination of inattention and theological ignorance on the part of members. I worked hard to communicate more clearly, and I tried to train people to listen theologically. I received my share of compliments on sermons, and I knew my insights were often excellent, but I also felt that many people failed to listen adequately and were not "getting" it. My frustration rose when I began campus ministry. Finally, as I neared my wit's end, students got through to me about shortening my sermons, saying less in a more focused way, being myself, and not trying so hard. I had had enough failure that I was ready to give up and try something different. I let go of some previous beliefs about the essentials of good preaching and my need to be a great preacher. I realized that the problem was not the listeners but my neglect to listen to the needs of the listeners. I believe the effectiveness of my sermons has increased as a result.

Disrupt Vicious Circles

A fourth skill of circular assessment is to avoid excessive analysis and to identify and highlight key feedback circles in the emotional system. Insight into why things have gone as they have is not always necessary or helpful. What is most important is that the "vicious circles" are interrupted and replaced by "virtuous circles," and that life moves along in a developmentally appropriate way. We do not have to figure everything out. It is enough to find one or a few key stuck points and identify the faulty attempts at a solution so that we can seek a different outcome. In fact, sometimes it does not matter whether we know what is "causing" the problem, so long as we can assess what works as a solution or as first steps in that direction. Take, for example, the congregation that seemed stuck in a habit of unfriendliness and gossip about the pastor. There was no obvious issue of conflict or discontent, and no one could pinpoint the problem. The fellowship committee sponsored a series of mini-potlucks involving the pastor and various subgroups of the congregation so that people and the pastor and his family could get to know each other. The emotional atmosphere of the congregation warmed up without any agreement on what the "cause" had been.

Admit When You're Stumped

A fifth skill of circular assessment is to admit when you are stumped. Sometimes those who practice Strategic and Brief family therapy will admit the near-impossibility of change, or admit they are stymied, as a paradoxical tactic. I do this often in therapy and occasionally in pastoral work, because I know that admitting powerlessness often leads us toward solutions. It is not merely a technique. Sometimes I really cannot fathom what is going on or how to solve it. I am convinced that a helper cannot, and probably should not, solve many problems alone for someone else. I do not recommend dishonesty in employing such a tactic, but it can be used honestly in the awareness that it is powerful.

Admitting that you are stumped, or that you may be able to help with only a small part of the problem, may prompt your clients or members to take more initiative to solve their own problem. Your admission may send a message of belief in their own problem-solving resources. It may even begin to break through a subtle power struggle in which part of the hidden agenda was to defeat the therapist or pastor. One hidden motive may be to get the helper finally to validate the client's pain and perception of the dilemma's depth and complexity. If the therapist or pastor confirms this perception and gives up, the contest may no longer be an issue. The therapist and clients, or pastor and people, may finally be able to join the same team and work together. Sometimes therapy clients turn the tables and try to prove the therapist wrong by showing that they are not helpless and can solve their problem. Either way, everybody wins.

It is possible in most cases for constructive change to begin before a pastor, leader, or church group is crushed and driven to a point of feeling helpless, hopeless, and worthless. We can confess our inability to change matters by ourselves without despairing. The important thing is to let go and admit our limits, individually and corporately.

Change does not depend totally on us. After all, God is at work in churches and synagogues. Sometimes for pastors and self-identified prophets, the danger is that we, like the prophet Jonah when he preached repentance to Ninevah, become so angry and negative about the people's seeming lack of response that we do not notice when God begins to work repentance in the group and the situation begins to change. Our failure to notice and fan these sparks of the Spirit may contribute to the stuckness. Sometimes in assessment and problem-solving, the kind of humbling and repentance required of leaders is simply to start believing that God is at work in our midst, even if we do not see it, and to bring people together in a way that gives the Spirit a chance to unleash the changes already in process.

Leading Circular Assessment

Once we are working on these five skills, we are ready to lead a "circular" or "systemic" assessment process among leaders to size up the situation and to decide the most helpful way to define the problems.

Conducted properly, circular assessment can begin to free up a system.
A circular process stands in contrast to a "linear process," which would
go straight to a simple conclusion, leaving out perspectives and information surrounding the problem. Linear assessment processes often play
right into scapegoating and other forms of stuckness because they fail to
see the bigger picture of interrelated behaviors. Circular assessment involves four primary phases led by a counselor or facilitator:

- Building the assessment leadership circle.
- Building the complainant circle by drawing in relevant people.
- Building the problem-solving circle of leaders, complainants, and
  other participants.
- Creating an assessment by encircling the problem and defining it so
  that we can solve it together.

In each of these dimensions of teamwork, the crucial elements are
an awareness of systemic forces and the way we construct our social
reality together, plus an inclusiveness that values each perspective and
sees solutions emerging from the synthesis of views and teamwork. Some
of the circle-building is a matter of getting to know one another, putting
agendas and viewpoints on the table, and agreeing on rules of procedure.
Three specific skills are essential: circular questions, humility about
"objectivity," and avoidance of cross-generational coalitions.

In writing about stuck congregations, I have stressed the part denial
plays in problems and the importance of acknowledging feelings. Even
so, I must warn against implicitly crediting the content of an unsubstan-
tiated complaint by immediately treating it as fact. Sometimes focusing
on a difficulty does magnify it into a problem. Sometimes it is healthier
to focus on subtle and not-so-subtle signs of God's healing and renewing. Sometimes it is most productive to focus attention on the exceptions
and the spontaneous solutions that have gone unnoticed, and to fan these
sparks. Such intentional shifting of group attention is not the same as
denial. The problem is recognized, but it is not allowed to control our
attention, to define who we are, or to limit God's actions in our midst.

Build the Leadership Circle

Three basic stages serve to build the assessment leadership team:

- Decide whom to include in the executive circle for making the assessment.
- Solidify the executive circle.
- Build the broader leadership circle; i.e., include relevant leaders from outside the executive circle.

Deciding who will make an assessment is not always obvious. If you are the pastor or lay leader of a congregation, it is probably appropriate that you initiate thinking through who should assess the situation. Whether it is best to work alone or with a co-leader depends on the situation and on your style of operating. If you can recall which approach, "going solo" or involving others, has been tried unsuccessfully in the past, then you may be better off trying the other approach or some variation of it.

It is generally preferable at the earliest stages of the assessment process to involve as many people as possible who can shed light on the problem. If only two people have been involved in a problem or difficulty (and the matter is not a criminal offense), the problem may be best assessed and handled by only those two and a mediator. Most of the time, however, others will have been triangled or hooked into the emotional process. They will influence the process outside your awareness unless you include them in the official process. Involving others gives you and them a chance to hear multiple perspectives, to assign roles that can be coordinated, and to multiply and leverage efforts. In this individualistic culture, the genuine development of teamwork in problem solving is, more often than not, the new and different pattern. Often teamwork is an expression of the kinds of relationships and process we seek when we talk about getting unstuck.

In family therapy, counselors can work with the most motivated family member even if other family members refuse to come to therapy. They can find ways to work with whatever and whoever is available.

But if therapists can get both parents, plus the children and perhaps even extended family members to come, a tremendous advantage accrues. They can go around the circle and hear a variety of perspectives on the problem and its solution. They can observe how family members interact with the therapist and each other. One learns what solutions have been tried and what the clients think might work. One can contract with each person as to their goals for the therapy and what outcome would satisfy them. Then energies can be harnessed toward these goals or a single goal that emerges when perspectives are combined. Everyone can be persuaded to agree to ground rules. The therapist can begin to reframe the situation and weave the family members together in the teamwork they will need to solve their problems.

In many cases, this process in the first session of including and validating each member's perspective, goals, and feelings is a major intervention that differs from past patterns. The family may never before have had each perspective heard and acknowledged by anyone vested with authority. Some family members most likely have never really heard the other members' thoughts and feelings.

Pastors who do the same sort of team building in the congregation among leaders may be well on the way to getting unstuck. After all the sophisticated talk about systemic therapy and paradoxical interventions, the bottom line is that people need to feel that they are heard, that their feelings are acknowledged, and that they are being taken seriously and appreciated for who they are. They need to feel that they are treated fairly and justly, in a way appropriate to creatures who bear God's image. That is both the simple truth and the difficult task of healers and leaders. When our systemic arrangements and style of communication foster emotional justice, not just for us but for everyone, then we are unstuck. If we get such teamwork going, we are at least halfway there, if not home free.

Who will do the assessment is the first question to answer in building the leadership team. As we build the assessment leadership circle, it is usually crucial to focus first on teamwork among the congregation's executive leadership, particularly the pastors and elected congregational officers. I have seen many congregations stuck at this point because the pastors and other leaders were not emotionally supportive of each other. In most such cases, council leaders could not back the pastor but were not honest about it, or they were caught up in the hidden emotional agendas of individuals outside the formal leadership.

Family therapists are generally aware of the importance of the primary alliance between the parents or adult leaders of the family. If the parents get their act together, the benefits will extend to the children. However, in emotional systems like families and congregations, official, formally elected leaders do not always function as the true leaders or "parents." It is important to go beyond the formal executive team and build a broader leadership and assessment team that includes other key formal and informal leaders. Informal leaders in the emotional system are often best equipped to interpret what is going on and what will or will not fly in the congregation. If we fail to include these informal leaders or try to fight them, the problem-solving process may be undermined. How much better if we can win their partnership, either informally or by officially inviting them to help. Such inclusion may enhance both their informal leadership and our official leadership.

Build the Complainant Circle

Complainants included in an assessment circle can be dealt with constructively in a way unlikely to occur if they complain only behind the scenes. The spirit of a circular process involves giving each person or group a voice and an equal hearing. It is important not to allow one or a few angry people to dominate the discussion by talking too much or by remaining silent and hiding their position to gain a power advantage. A skillful leader will draw some out, put limits on others, and make sure the spirit of a circular meeting prevails. It is especially important to hear from those who have not been allowed a voice. If we do not give a voice to the functional "children" (members who have no formal or informal leadership role, those without much power in the system, and those who are usually left out), we will lose a valuable and often crucial perspective. This does not mean that we need to hear from every individual in a congregation, only from representatives of each subgroup so that each emotional perspective is heard. The flaws in our assessment (as well as the flaws in our attempted solutions) can often be traced to omitting significant voices or perspectives. Congregations are not meant only to have a choir but to *be* a "choir," with every voice needed, blended, and balanced.

Build the Problem-Solving Circle

The problem-solving circle includes the leadership circle, the complainant circle and any other people brought in as resources to help to assess
and solve the problem. The main point is to build the group with an
orientation toward solutions, avoiding the assumption of an oppositional
relationship between complainants and leaders (with other members
feeling they must either take sides or remove themselves to the fringes).
It can help to make the point that we are in this together as a team and
that we want an assessment that leads to a solution all can celebrate.
Even members with very little involvement can be invited to support the
effort with words of encouragement, prayers, and potentially helpful
input. Once this broad spirit of teamwork is fostered, it is not difficult
to think of other specific practical methods to build the team.

Circling the Problem

The kinds of questions we ask shape the process and the answers we get.
Working with these components, circular process asks what family therapists call "circular questions." The kinds of questions we usually ask
are "linear." Linear questions start with an hypothesis, often assuming
blame or identifying a single cause, and then seek to find evidence to
prove the hypothesis. Sometimes linear investigators hide these hypoth-
eses or are unaware of them and subtly influence the direction of the
process by the questions they ask. Investigated by such questioning, one
may feel manipulated by what purports to be an objective process. Linear
questions are manipulative. They seek linear causes and strive to confirm hunches about the major cause or who is to blame. Such an approach cannot paint a picture of circular causation or find a practical
solution that serves and respects all.
      Investigation using circular questions is more authentically open-
minded. Often, as in teaching, circular questions ("What came first, the
chicken or the egg?") are intended more to broaden people's minds than
to narrow the focus to single answers. These questions assume circular
causation. They implicitly challenge our usual beliefs about single,
mechanical, linear, sequential, close-in-time causes and effects. If hy-
potheses arise in circular questioning, they are seen as tentative and

pragmatic rather than as establishing one "truth." An explanation could start equally well at any point in the circle. The real issue is the way the parts interact to keep the circle or feedback loop going, not who started it or who plays the biggest role. Blame has no place in circular questioning, only shared responsibility.

Consequently, people tend to experience circular questions as inviting, nonthreatening, nonmanipulative, and fair. If your questioning does not seem to others to have these qualities, perhaps you should ask yourself if you have a secret agenda that manipulates their answers, if you are hinting at blame, or if you are probing intrusively. While defensiveness may be based on suspicion from past experience with linear questioners, it may also be a legitimate reaction to the style of questioning. Linear investigators who try to solve congregations' problems may feel that they mean well and are legitimate rescuers. But in my experience, they are usually part of the problem rather than of the solution, especially when they are oblivious to their manipulative influence.

What we call "cause" and what we call "effect" are known to be a product of how we carve up the joints of reality. When we use circular questioning, we accept responsibility for our punctuating of reality. We know our questions will either open or close doors. So we try to ask questions that will multiply possibilities and lead to more livable solutions. We use open-ended questions and questions that lead to behavioral, interactive descriptions:

- "What happens? How do things go?"
- "When they do that, what do you do?"
- "What came just before that? And before that? And before that?"
- "What happened next? and next? and next?"
- "What was going on with others then?"
- "If I were a fly on the wall, what would I see?"
- "What is your perspective? And yours? And yours?"
- "How would things look different if this problem were solved?"
- "When things were better, what was happening then to make them better?"

These questions go all around the problem and the group, asking about the situation in different ways rather than in one way. They do not imply one specific answer. People are asked for concrete behavioral

observations. In family therapy, they are asked to refrain from interpreting the behaviors. In a therapy process, I may invite interpretations at
first so that I can learn the "position" from which people are coming and
use this information later. Then I will be better able to phrase interventions in terms of their standpoint and gain better cooperation. But most
of the time, I block interpretations because they imply blame or focus
fruitlessly on interpreting others' interior motives.

It is helpful to establish rules early in the process about not blaming,
not reading others' minds or interpreting their motives, and focusing on
self instead of the other. Otherwise less constructive rules that reinforce
the problem may become the norm. "The way we've always done it"
tends to develop its own momentum which, like an ocean liner, is hard
to turn around once it gets up a head of steam. Circular questions tend to
establish constructive rules right away without confrontation.

Whatever interventions and rules are used at this stage, the astute
listener/observer will be gathering information about the behavior and
the system that surrounds the problem. The outcome of making sure that
everyone gives his or her version is a complex description incorporating
multiple perspectives. The objective is not a "factual" description but
rather a three-dimensional picture that is closer to reality. The process
should draw us all into the reality we describe and the hoped-for future
so that our reality begins to be creatively transformed. Granted, pastors
and lay leaders are not therapists, but they can profitably apply the same
kind of circular assessment as they look at a congregation's problems
and difficulties.

The Myth of Objectivity

Most of us are prone to several primary errors in this sort of process
because we are ingrained with cultural biases that are oversimplified
and linear. Chief among these errors is the "myth of objectivity," which
includes believing that problem-solving team leaders are completely
"objective" and therefore not part of the whole circle of the problem,
and believing that the main goal of assessment is to uncover objective
"facts," which are the "real truth" and exist independently of our inquiry. Systemic therapists today recognize that the belief that we can
attain objectivity is myth. This myth has helped science achieve great

discoveries, but it has blinded and crippled science in other ways. We now know from atomic science and other fields that not only observer bias but also the very act of observation changes the context to influence what is observed.

In one congregation several young members complained that the youth group was stuck and in decline. They did not directly blame Katie, the youth worker, but they implied that there were serious problems with her. They could not define the problem but asked for a full investigation to "save" this group. The president and vice president of the congregation took on the investigation to "get to the bottom" of the problem. With great sincerity and sacrifice of time they attempted to gather information as objectively as possible. They held private interviews with all relevant people they could identify, attempting to withhold judgment and refrain from voicing opinions during the process.

As the process unfolded, Katie became more and more anxious, wondering what was being said, how her words had been taken by the investigators, what the youths' real concerns and motives were, and why the process was initiated without her endorsement. Some interviewees told her they had felt uncomfortable with the investigators' questions, which seemed to force them into "for or against" responses and failed to encompass the whole picture.

After several weeks Katie became increasingly anxious and depressed. She had been interviewed initially but not included after that point, even after new information emerged for her to share. The investigators felt they might lose objectivity if they allowed her too much input and participation. They also noticed that she was not functioning well in her role and seemed a bit paranoid and defensive. They saw this behavior as evidence and confirmation of the complaints. They believed they were getting to the bottom of the situation and that the process had been fair and objective. They did not see that their granting greater weight to the complainants' request for an investigation than to Katie's opposition to it had already compromised fairness and influenced the youth worker's reaction. They did not ask how she felt about the process or how their own style of questioning influenced what they saw. Thus they could not realize that their solution was part of the problem.

What safeguards could have made this process more circular and less likely to aggravate the problem? First, the belief in "objectivity" and "fact-finding" should have been replaced by the goals of fairness, faithfulness, shared responsibility, and solvability in creating a portrait of the problem. Second, the leaders should have given Katie a significant role in creating and continuing to shape the process of inquiry.

Cross-Generational Coalitions

By excluding Katie and allowing the youth and the board to define the context, the leaders participated in a second common assessment error, what we have referred to as a "cross-generational coalition." This phenomenon develops in a family when one parent or grandparent sides with a child and opposes or excludes the other parent, or they team up to "help" the other parent as if he or she were a child. The process implicitly reverses the roles of leadership and responsibility. A child or children (or those in a role functionally similar to that of children in a family) are given leadership responsibility and power which should belong to a "parent" role. The parent is reduced to the functional role of a child or of outsider to the family. Some family therapists see this confusion of hierarchy as the most common way that families create bigger problems in trying to solve difficulties. A cross-generational coalition attempts to solve a problem at the wrong level. The solution skips the appropriate generational level where the alliance should be forged. People are put into paradoxical binds—the parent has to be the "child," and the child has to be the "parent." The pay-off may please a child who likes to wield power and a parent who wants to avoid responsibility, but it is ultimately debilitating to both.

Such a cross-generational coalition began from the start of the process in Katie's situation, largely because the investigators thought objectivity and neutrality meant giving Katie and each of the complainers equal input. Ironically, this attempt at neutrality not only prevented Katie from having the degree of influence appropriate to her role; it prevented her from having even equal input. The leaders were so "caring" and "concerned" toward the youth that they were hooked into a bias from the start.

In family therapy, we find that parents often fail to realize that the basis of caring effectively for their children is to keep the parental leadership team primary and well coordinated. They think that by putting the child above the parental team building they are helping the child—which is seldom the case.

This does not mean that parents (or congregational executive teams) have to agree on everything or maintain a "united front" that denies their differences. Cross-generational emotional coalitions can form even in the face of a pretense of parental agreement and mutual support. Such coalitions are then all the more crazy-making because of the cover-up. Honest and open treatment of differences often prevents cross-generational coalitions, or at least makes them easier to deal with.

Honest differences can even strengthen teamwork, exemplify healthy conflict, and offer an enriched variety of perspectives for the children. There are many ways to have a healthy family or congregation. All of them tend to validate each person and include each in appropriate ways. This means that power and leadership responsibility are assigned in ways commensurate with each person's abilities and his or her role in the family or congregation.

As in this example with Katie, I have seen associate or assistant pastors (often women) put into situations in which they were functionally treated as children. Often those in the "parental" role were not conscious of the condescending, patronizing style of their "caring" and its effect on other adults.

In one situation a senior pastor and congregational president (both successful, white, middle-class males) arranged a process of evaluation and accountability for the female associate pastor. A pastor from outside the congregation confronted them with their patronizing, top-down style and suggested that it was implicitly sexist and would not help bring out the best in any professional woman. The male leaders, perhaps reacting to the politically loaded accusation, vehemently denied that sexism was involved and hinted that no one could work with this woman. They refused to consider the matter further. Many subsequent deliberations went on privately or at meetings from which the associate was excluded. Eventually she resigned under pressure in a hush-hush atmosphere. Confused and wounded, the congregation remained stuck for a long time afterward.

Unless congregations unlearn this patronizing and secretive problem-solving approach, we will be stuck in mega-problems with systemic political overtones involving not only feminists but also every newly empowered group that has been enraged by self-serving condescension in the past. A truly circular process of assessment and problem-solving includes members appropriately but does not engage in cross-generational coalitions or alliances with members, leaders, or staff that exclude other staff and treat them like children.

The way we assess and define a problem can make it bigger and more entrenched, or it can start us well on the way to getting unstuck. Try to establish, both by explicit agreements and by the way you carry out the process, rules that are open, flexible, affirming and fair, that include people at a level appropriate to their role in the congregation, and that build teamwork and cooperation in a circular, inclusive style. Taking these steps will set the stage for a solution.

Questions

1. What methods does your congregation have for hearing complaints and validating feelings without being controlled by negative people?

2. How does your congregation define its problems? Is the process more formal or informal? Circular or linear?

3. What kinds of behavioral problem cycles can you see in your congregation? What part do you and other leaders play in perpetuating these cycles? Are there ways you could "give up" or admit powerlessness that might help disrupt these cycles?

4. How might you go about doing a circular assessment of your congregation? Whom would you include, and what types of questions would you ask?

5. How solid is your executive leadership team? Are there any secret cross-generational coalitions undermining the solidity of this team?

CHAPTER 10

Prevention of Stuckness

The most important thing we can do to prevent stuckness in the church is to use more circular processes. "Circular" is a good practical synonym for "systemic" because it creates an image that stimulates the imagination and energizes us. All kinds of experiences and processes, from turning wheels to windmills to dancing, involve circles that not only revolve but also generate energy or accomplish a useful purpose. In relation to the word "circular," think of these characteristics of the new paradigm:

- Seeing reality is always in process rather than static.
- Valuing diversity.
- Affirming partnership and mutuality.
- Embracing paradoxes.
- Opening and encouraging life-giving feedback loops.
- Living webs of interconnection and interdependence.

Organic, systemic processes are dynamic, curvy, diverse, interdependent, spiraling, embracing both/and, going back to go forward, growing, flowing, and developing through time.

Leaders in the new paradigm must learn to use a more systemic style to help congregations stay unstuck. They must learn the paradox that we need to lead in curves and circles to move forward.

Leading in Circles

Much thinking about leadership is linear. It is imagined that the leader gets up front and pulls, or gets behind and pushes people in a straight line toward a goal or vision. Thinking about leadership in linear imagery does not, however, lend itself to shared responsibility, partnership, and mutuality, or to healing and sustainable energy flow. What is worse, pushing and pulling organic systems tend to result in their pushing or pulling back in the opposite direction.

Circular leadership in the church or synagogue respects the organic processes of adjustment and growth and gives special attention to healing processes. Grief is a circular or spiral healing process, and we often, paradoxically, must lead a congregation back into the grief or conflict to bring sufficient emotional closure that it can get unstuck. We have seen how often we must encircle both sides of a paradox to get free of a bind. We have also seen that information flow and feedback loops should be opened up and encouraged to swirl through the congregation and the surrounding community. This motion may seem chaotic to some, but such "chaos," paradoxically, may be necessary to displace destructive underground triangles and gossip and to create positive trust and momentum. The image of circularity can serve as a generative metaphor to help us think through more systemically how we might "do church" differently in life-giving ways.

Brainstorming

Brainstorming is an excellent example of a circular or spiral process. It lays out rules to create a safe environment for risk (e.g., no idea is too wild, and no idea is to be criticized while brainstorming). It is time-limited but also part of a larger planning process. It includes everyone's input. Ideas feed off other ideas and create new energy and forward momentum through positive feedback loops that spiral out. It is important that ideas and participation be affirmed and that critique be blocked from this process, lest it burst every bubble of new energy. Explaining why an idea will not work, sneering at it because it is odd or unrealistic, or demanding that people justify their ideas kills the circular process quickly. There are other times and places to evaluate and make difficult choices. It is also important that, once accomplished, a brainstorming session not be considered a finished process with closed-off conclusions or firm commitments. Brainstorming is a matter of creating a safe space that sanctifies off-the-wall, crazy-sounding ideas, blesses ridiculous connections, and encourages playful imagination. These are precisely values we need in the church to enrich our life together, to break out of problems in which we are stuck, and to discern a vision of mission that empowers us for ministry together.

Besides specific brainstorming sessions, we ought to provide other occasions to tap gifts such as differentness, childlike imagination, uniqueness, risk-taking courage, "craziness," playfulness, curiosity, experimental spirit, and challenging behaviors. Examples might be special experimental worship services, award ceremonies to honor unusual gifts, talent shows, mission idea festivals, creativity contests, "challenge-to-the-church dialogues," dramatic celebrations of congregational history events, including especially overlooked female or minority saints, assignment of roles for children and the developmentally disabled, establishment of roles on congregational boards such as officers of diversity, playfulness/humor, prophetic challenge, and creativity. We also ought to make the most of such cutting-edge ministries as world missions, intercultural ministries, ecumenical ministries, and campus ministries. Such ministries can often catalyze brainstorming and creative energy for other parts of the religious community. Circular leadership draws a wider circle of resources in to help stimulate the flow of creativity.

Circular Visioning

I especially recommend ample use of brainstorming as part of a larger circular visioning process. Much stuckness in regard to mission is rooted in a lack of vision or, more often, in a lack of shared vision. Some congregations fight fruitlessly about a host of details and secondary issues or go nowhere in mission because they fail to reach the underlying vision issues. In some cases, congregations address vision issues but do so in such a linear or top-down manner that too many people and resources are excluded and the vision never catches the congregation's imagination.

Applying circularity might mean the following:

- Make sure the brainstorming group is diverse and includes both men and women of various ages, temperaments, racial and ethnic backgrounds, and experience. For the larger visioning process of

the congregation, we need circular and inclusive brainstorming
sessions, lest our vision end up narrow, static, or exclusive.

- Do not restrict brainstorming to what seems realistic or possible.
Brainstorming is an occasion for expanding circles. A time will
come later to zero in, to create targets, and to mark boundaries. The
more expansive ideas generated may help focus these targets later,
put them in context, and relate them meaningfully to a larger aim.

- Do not restrict brainstorming to the future. Circle back and embrace
memories. Let these memories and stories trigger and evoke new
ideas. Cultivate the sense that God's calling for the future both
grows out of our past and extends beyond it.

- Discover and use strengths of the congregation, but also use negatives. Seek ways to reframe weaknesses and failures so that they
point to strengths and resources for the vision. For example, a
congregation that has survived much grief, loss, or hardship may
have a special ability to minister to other suffering individuals and
congregations. What might otherwise seem an occasion for shame
and cover-up may be grasped as a gift from God and integrated into
the congregation's vision of mission and ministry.

While the leader plays a crucial role in envisioning the future, the
emergent sense and synergy of the process, not the leader's self-gener-
ated enthusiasm alone, give heart-capturing power to a vision and create
the sense that it is a gift and a calling from God.

In linear visioning, a leader brings a vision and then tries to sell it,
impose it, or sneak it in on the congregation. In circular visioning, as in
linear visioning, the pastor with the highest level of responsibility plays
a central role in developing a shared vision and must enthusiastically
and effectively "sell" it. The vision must live in the pastor's heart if it is
to live in the shared heart of pastor and congregation, but that does not
mean that the pastor brings it from outside the congregation. The vision
may be sown in the pastor's heart by seeds from the congregation, or
seeds from elsewhere may germinate in the systemic soil of that congregation's relationship with the pastor.

How do we collect these seeds? R. Paul Stevens, dean of Regent
College in Vancouver, British Columbia, and Phillip Collins, principal
of Carey Theological College, also in Vancouver, share a helpful idea in
their book *The Equipping Pastor*.[1] They suggest that the pastor hand out

pieces of paper to all members at worship and ask them to write down what they would like their congregation to do in mission if money were no object. That is a simple and creative example of how to collect pieces of a vision. Small groups are another obvious place to gather seeds, to share the vision as it evolves, to collect feedback to shape it into a more powerful shared vision, and to foster growing enthusiasm. In addition, from an intergenerational viewpoint, it is important to make listening pastoral visits to members who have deeper roots in the congregation and fulfill an important function in its emotional system, especially wise elders. From them, one may discern how future vision may incorporate their vision from the past without getting stuck in it.

Circular processes also cast a large net to gather hopes and dreams. This net may reach into the wider community and include perspectives of former and inactive members and of the unchurched. What would inspire and draw them? Linear processes tend to do things once in one way and then move on quickly. A circular visioning process will come at data-gathering from a number of angles, will not fear gathering too many pieces to throw into the vision "stew," and will take time and use creative imagination to honor the past.

If we do not talk about the past, we may repeat its mistakes. Unhealed, silenced pain or conflict resurfaces in one form or another until we hear and heed its voice. Unlearned lessons from failures lead to similar failures. Shameful sins kept secret continue to haunt and control our lives. When we refuse to speak of significant departed ones, they continue to exert their influence through invisible loyalties, often unrecognized and unavailable to be fairly challenged. If we fail to honor the past and especially if we put down those who served before us, even when it appears that they were unfaithful in some way, we may be stuck, unable to come up with a new vision and spirit. We usually do not need to linger long, but the past must be honored, forgiven, and reframed so that it is integrated and opens toward our shared future. Then the circle is completed sufficiently and can spiral toward a new and motivating shared vision.

Circular Call Process

Another circular approach used in some congregations is a circular call process. Some call processes are controlled by a small group with minimal input from the rest of the congregation, except for the views of a few key people. These call committees are task-oriented and eager to get the job done. Usually they follow a linear process and disband once they have found a new pastor.

I recently observed a circular call process. Call committee members represented the variety of major viewpoints in the congregation. The group was fairly balanced by sex and age. The committee chair acted as a leader among equals who shared control of the process.

The agreed-upon rules were circular. Group members agreed to take all the time needed to listen to the congregation, to listen to one another, to work through their disagreements to consensus, and to discern the Spirit's leading. It was agreed that most decisions were negotiable, and if anyone became uncomfortable with a decision later, the group would revisit it and seek a new consensus. Circular process requires time, patience, and often an explicit commitment to take intuition and subtle feelings seriously.

The committee used a circular data-gathering process. Group members talked extensively with many parishioners and staff. They compiled questionnaire results. They held congregational meetings. They initiated meetings with every program group in the congregation. They intentionally sought a continual, inclusive stream of feedback. They also kept people in touch with their progress through newsletters, forums, and call committee updates at worship services. They welcomed questions and additional input throughout.

The result of this open, inclusive process was first a new sense of community and depth of relationship among committee members, which transcended their differences and conflicting personal agendas. The second result was the selection of a pastor whose circular leadership style was well suited to the congregation's needs. Part of the call's credibility rested on the thoroughness of the process. After give-and-take negotiating, including a clear agreement about expectations and limits, the pastor accepted the call. Such conviction and clarity can prevent later confusion and stuckness, especially if the resulting informal emotional contract as well as the formal contract are widely communicated and "owned" by the congregation.

It is best, in terms of circular process, to keep continuity of support, feedback, and teamwork between such a committee and the pastor. Most linear-process call committees consider their goal accomplished, disband abruptly, pass the responsibility to another board without much communication, and make no allowance for an ongoing evolution of the original formal and informal emotional contract. This lack of continuity leads to potential misunderstandings and often breaks off the sense of circular partnership that began in this crucial "courtship" phase.

Circular Evaluation Process

Another application of circular process is in evaluation or review. I have experienced this style in two situations. One was Clinical Pastoral Education, in which an ongoing process of feedback was interspersed with occasional larger evaluations. It involved learning contracts; peer-group supervision, evaluation and feedback; plus respectful supervision from more experienced professionals. Trainees received much feedback about their pastoral work with people in crisis.

I have also experienced a good circular review process in campus ministry. Note that the review must be planned and scheduled. Sudden, surprise evaluations are rarely balanced or inclusive. A carefully chosen panel interviews a wide variety of people over a two-day period. The pastor follows guidelines to set up interviews with individuals and groups that represent aspects of the campus community and the campus ministry.

The panel that leads the review is comprised of a campus ministry official, a clergy representative from the bishop's office, a lay synod representative, and a campus pastor from another campus. The pastor writes a self-evaluation and is interviewed. Support staff, area pastors, the campus ministry board, local campus ministry colleagues, faculty, administration, involved and uninvolved students, the pastor's spouse—all are interviewed. A full circle of perspectives is sought. Questions come from various angles and seek to clarify positive and negative aspects of the pastor's functioning and of the whole ministry.

In interviews, the panel often tries to suggest by their questions how others can support the pastor's ministry and relate to the campus ministry. They seek to clarify vision and networking possibilities for the future. At the conclusion, the panel draws together a composite picture with commendations and recommendations and presents it to the campus pastor. Provision is made for follow-up on any recommendations for change.

Pastors rarely get such credible and balanced feedback. The process tends also to be affirming. I have found it moving to know that at least a few people have gathered this degree of knowledge of my work and appreciate my strengths.

The most circular and systemic evaluation processes make clear that not only the pastor is being evaluated but also the staff, lay leaders, members, the formal structure of the system, and informal systemic arrangements. Performance occurs in a context, and whatever people see in their pastor has much to do with their own attitudes and behavior, the systemic context, the habits of the relationship, and the mesh of expectations. This context must be clearly implied in the way a review is set up, questions asked, feedback given, and recommendations carried out. If the process is circular at all these levels, it can be powerful in getting and keeping the system unstuck. If it is not circular, the same old implicit blaming and nonsystemic focus on the pastor may surface to keep the congregation stuck.

Circular Use of Denominational Officials

One problem with bringing in denominational officials to evaluate a situation or resolve a conflict is that they do not always understand circular process or have the skills and the time to carry it out. They often have an emotionally overwhelming job without realistic focus and limits, and without much feedback or support. Their jobs are often riddled with binds that frustrate and confuse. In addition, they may have limited first-hand knowledge of current developments in a given congregation. Add to this a number of political dynamics, and we have a recipe for the judicatory official's getting emotionally hooked and creating more of a problem.

In the new-paradigm church we need to find and use people who have the systemic skills and the time and energy to conduct circular processes with congregations stuck in conflict. Sometimes uniquely gifted or specially trained denominational representatives can assume this role.

I know several denominational officials who are moving toward a partnership paradigm. In many cases, it is so difficult for a judicatory official to apply circular processes of assessment and intervention that looking to denominational staff for this service may be unfair and unrealistic.

Circular Teaching and Fellowship

Circular process can take place at any level of the church or other religious institution. A leader I know who exemplifies circular leadership in much of his work evokes the gifts of others, connects them, reminds them of the resources they already have, and helps them grieve the loss of the past so that they can go on with the future. In a recent workshop he led, some were at first disappointed that he did not give more answers as the guest "expert." What he did instead was to divide us into small groups, sitting at round tables. He gave us focus questions to discuss and followed up with full group gatherings where we shared the small groups' insights. He then lifted up the group insights and used some to get at points he hoped would emerge. He lectured some, but even then did not present his thoughts as those of an expert. He shared himself and called us back to the best of the ecumenical Christian tradition to carry into the future.

Small groups are a well-known part of circular process in many congregations. Effective congregations usually have many meaningful small groups so that all members may connect to one or more of them. These congregations also have the sense that the small groups are connected and encircled by the larger worshipping, serving congregational community.

Sometimes circularity is an almost ridiculously simple matter of such spatial arrangements as table shapes, room shapes, and staff office arrangements. I know of a church whose trouble with staff communication seemed at least partially traceable to architecture. The offices were separated and scattered in a long line. Triangles tended to form among those whose offices were in close proximity. In other cases, I have seen office arrangements where boundaries were clear but where staff also talked more often and openly. They bumped into each other a good deal, and it was hard to talk without other staff noticing. It is less likely that triangles or clique-ish "pseudo-circles" will form in more open circular spatial arrangements.

One pastor told me about a fight that erupted in her church over one

group's desire to purchase round tables. A woman whom the pastor characterized as "holding the church emotionally hostage" refused to let
them depart from the old rectangular tables. You do not have to have
round tables to have circular processes. Yet what an apt symbol of the
power struggle between the two paradigms!

Circular Self Defense

When we apply circular process to a pastor's or church leader's responses to attack, the analogy to the Eastern martial arts is apt. Arts of
self-defense such as judo and aikido teach practitioners to use and redirect the attacker's energy to throw him. These arts also focus on strategic methods such as using leverage and the tender, vulnerable points
of the attacker to disable and neutralize the attack. An even more circular style is used in the ancient Chinese discipline of t'ai chi. Here the
gentle but powerful circular movements of animals and nature are emu-
lated for the sake of emotional and spiritual health and to enhance energy. If a stranger were to strike at or bump into a t'ai chi practitioner, the
latter might roll off the blow in circular fashion rather than rigidly resisting. Thus, it would be no blow at all but simply a gentle, cooperative
turning in harmony with the movement of the other and with nature.
    We need not be naive about evil or its desire to deceive, dominate,
and destroy us. Circular self-defense is more a matter of learning a
deeper form of power and self-defense. Paradoxical strategies and circular responses can surround, dodge, circle around behind, counter,
deflect, and even use and rechannel attacking energy. For example,
when someone has become vicious and devious in attitude and behavior
toward a pastor, directly confronting that person in a fit of anger, whether in private or in the presence of others, can play into the purposes of
the devious one. For this one to provoke the pastor or make the pastor
look bad renders the original accusations more credible to others unaware of the emotional context or the subtle provocations.
    One skilled in paradoxical techniques might be able to take a one-
down position, play dumb, admit helplessness, exaggerate how right the
attacker is, or make exaggerated excuses for him or her until others begin to articulate that the attacker's behavior is unacceptable. A leader
might reframe the viciousness as fear, concern, or pain, and use the

opportunity to express empathy, or prescribe that attackers do even more of what they are doing. One might also take initiative to bring complaints out in the open so they cannot hide in secret triangles; invite others to a circle of discussion about how this person's behavior has hurt them; and find other ways to flush out, block, and rechannel the attacks. There is no one formula. Working paradoxically requires a general sense that, whichever natural reaction we tend to get stuck in, we probably need to do something 180 degrees different.

It is not a huge leap to connect this whole style of self-defense with Jesus' style of nondefensive self-defense. He used whatever was thrown at him to expose evil, to redirect attacks, and to control the meaning of the situation. The accusers tried to define him and the situation, but he retained the power to define himself and to allow God to control the meaning of events.

Christians, especially Christian leaders, should recognize that Christlike self-defense leaves no place for violent and dominating uses of power. We as pastors and congregational leaders have a responsibility to serve as models of nonviolent methods of self-defense. We must be prepared for the reality that obedience will lead to suffering as it did for Jesus. But we ought also be aware of a certain strategic sense about the right time in God's will to confront the powers and risk suffering. We should recognize that when we obey the commands of Matthew 5:38-44 to turn the other cheek, to walk the second mile, to love our enemies and do good to them, and to resist evil nonviolently, we obey not out of a perverse love of suffering or out of cowardice or naïvete but out of faith. This faith includes the confidence that, short-term appearances to the contrary notwithstanding, following Jesus' way of strategic nonviolence is the way of true power.

Circular Biblical Interpretation and Preaching

Circular approaches to Scripture and preaching can also help keep us unstuck. Our use of language and of the process of creating meaning affects powerfully whether we are bound and stuck or free and open to the flow of God's creative energies. Preachers, as public meaning-makers and "weavers of the story," have a special calling to proclaim the gospel and tell the story of God's saving action in a way that encircles, incorporates, liberates, and transforms the stories of our life in the congregation.

Circular preaching can embrace many styles and methods. Techniques that might express circular preaching include discussion and dialogue sermons inviting listeners' questions, stories, and insights; "debate sermons" between two or more preachers; story sermons; sermons in which the preacher steps out of the pulpit and walks among the congregation addressing listeners; and "midrashic" sermons that retell and reinterpret biblical stories or events for today. The specific technique is less important than the humanized and inclusive spirit that extends beyond a linear, rational, monological style. A circular approach to preaching opens new possibilities, stimulates the imagination, energizes, draws people in, and activates their creativity. It embodies an attitude and outlook on the Word and the listeners that is unafraid to risk. It reaches out, encircles the lives of listeners, and brings them into the story.

Circular preaching can powerfully set the tone for the whole church, fostering other circular processes and keeping energy flowing.

Stuck, Closed, and Blurred Circles

Linear processes, when they serve within a larger circular paradigm, can help circular processes have direction and form. The appropriate combination of linearity and circularity is conveyed by the image of a moving spiral. Without some linearity, circles too get stuck. Inner circles become cliques, and boundaries are blurred. To stay unstuck, we need emotional boundaries, a sense of sequence and limits, and a sense of developmental and purposeful movement beyond our inner circles.

Emotional and organic systemic processes must be respected as wholes—a notion that seems to suggest that we deal with the whole all at once. On the contrary, respecting a systemic whole often means to give it time and to take things in small, sequential steps that give the rest of the whole enough time to adjust. When I conduct brief therapy, I often slow people down, help them go back to basics in communicating, take a step at a time, and focus on a specific solvable problem. It is simply one of life's paradoxes that the effort to go too fast or to move in circles too large undermines truly circular process. It blurs boundaries, overwhelms, and confuses.

Once circular processes get going and people stick with them long enough to discover their benefits, they become self-reinforcing. One good circular process tends to lead to another.

Questions

1. How do members of your congregation respond to leadership that pushes or pulls to get movement? What long-range fruit does this linear style of leadership bear in your organization's development?

2. What are some of the priorities and preferred techniques of circular leadership?

3. Where are the circular processes in your congregation, and how can you give them emphasis?

4. What circular leadership approaches can help your congregation move ahead?

CHAPTER 11

Theological Blockbusters

Throughout this book, I have woven into the text several counterparadoxical teachings of the faith as I understand it, "theological blockbust-
ers," which free up the flow of God's love in our midst when they are
applied. My Lutheran Christian bias will be obvious here, but I hope
these paradoxes will make sense to you in your own language and tradition. Here are several of the most important counter-paradoxes:

1. The more we fight for complete control and grasp for it, the
deeper the binds we create and the tighter their hold on us. Freedom
comes through letting go and letting God. Faith is ultimately trust: We
trust that God is bringing about the divine will despite setbacks and that
God's will is loving and life-giving. We trust that even if we are not in
total control, all hell will not break loose: God's goodness will continue
to win out in the long run. If we believe this, we look at the world, the
church, and ourselves not as things that need to be dominated for their
own good but as living organisms with which we are to cooperate, to
share reciprocally, and to care respectfully to allow God's goodness to
emerge in and from them.

2. The more we try to simplify life into neat little boxes of either/or
and to make it fit some absolute standard, the more we choke and distort
it. All of life is an ambiguous mix. Even Christians, as the sixteenth-
century reformers put it, are "simultaneously saints and sinners." This
ambiguity leads to difficulties. It means that painful imperfections must
be faced and that one must choose among shades of gray. At the same
time, there is more slack, more flexibility, and more liberating possibility to reality.

Accepting the ambiguity of life can help us see that there are more "in-betweens" to choose from than most of us realize. It can help us see that we have more choices about how to frame our experiences and tell the stories that shape us. The fact that a church is, as some say, "loaded with hypocrites" does not mean that it does not also have humble servants of God or that these hypocrites are not also forgiven sinners. A congregation stuck in an anxiety-driven attempted solution that blocks the flow of God's love does not cease to be the Body of Christ. We may hate the church and love it at the same time. We may choose to accept the ambiguity of life and admit the negative, yet lift up the positive, life-giving side of the truth and let it have the last word.

3. We, though only creatures, are created in God's image. Blaming others for our problems may make us feel less burdened for a time, but blaming degrades us and keeps us from dealing with our real burdens. Taking appropriate responsibility enhances our dignity and frees us from heavier burdens. Being created in God's image does not give us the divine right to rule. It gives us a calling to care for creation as representatives of a God who goes to extremes to love and care for it and to lure it back into a loving relationship. We are called not only to care but also to share in creating with God the social realities that shape us. As Adam was invited by God to name the animals and to call his partner, we are to take responsibility to name the reality God gives us and to call to other human beings. This "calling," which is quite different from "naming," refers to the recognition and announcement of what God has created, and implies equality.

4. The harder we try to become spiritual, the less human we tend to be, and the less spiritual in the truest sense. The harder we try to rescue others, the less genuinely loving we tend to become because we put ourselves in the role of saviors rather than of fellow strugglers supporting one another. In Jesus Christ the divine dwells in the human. In him the image of God was embodied in the true human being. To become more rightly spiritual is not to become more angelic or disembodied. It is to become more Christlike and thus more embodied and more truly human. Insofar as we let go our grasp on trying to be divine messiahs, rescuers, and saviors of others and the church, we will be positioned to empty ourselves and take the form of a servant. In humility, in humor, in service to humanity and to the earth, we discover our true humanity and thus our reflection of God's image and of true spirituality.

The church will become truly unstuck and reflect Christ's image insofar as it quits trying to be angelic and messianic and becomes more genuinely human. What would it mean to be more human? Humility, humor, acceptance of limits, mutuality, interdependence with all creation, willingness to risk, playfulness, a holistic attitude, courage, and commitment to struggle toward understanding, to wrestle over our differences, to share our pain, to take responsibility to co-create our reality with God, and to hold others in the same grace of God as we are held— these are the marks of humanness highlighted in a systemic paradigm.

5. God's saving action is revealed in ways quite opposite to what we would expect by reason and common sense. The supreme example is the cross. God both communicates and intervenes in paradoxical ways at the most crucial points. Often the biggest battles with the greatest evil can be won only through the paradoxical working of genuine faith and obedient love. Evil may be wrong, but it is not stupid, at least not at its most powerful. It does not deal in honest, straightforward, and fair competition. It fights dirty and deceptively, using every clever, double-binding trick to trap us and rob us of our humanity and our eternal birthright. The cross of Jesus trumps evil not only because it is well-intentioned and sacrificial love, but also because it is strategic love. This pivotal act of salvation history involved the right act of obedient love at the right place and the right time to counter the binding attempts of the powers and principalities.

6. The harder we try to save ourselves, the more stuck we are. Salvation comes by grace alone. This, I believe, is the ultimate therapeutic paradox. It is the great "double-bind buster." When we try to solve our own problems, especially as they grow out of our broken relationship with God, we create bigger problems that get us stuck. Trying to justify our lives by our own perfectionism leads to destructive, binding paradoxes. Legalism, the effort to keep God's law perfectly enough to deserve salvation, is a trap. "The letter kills, but the spirit gives life" (2 Cor. 3:6b). The law is good, but it kills because we are deceived into thinking that we can solve our deepest problems by ourselves, if we just try harder. The paradox that frees and gives life is that, while our efforts will never be enough, God's grace is enough. By grace, God has given all the solutions we need, despite our sins. Ours is but to receive through faith. When this freeing paradox is received, it will release us from trying harder and getting more stuck. It will break us out of totalistic demands and double binds that have held us captive and blocked the

healing, transforming, energizing flow of God's love through us, individually and corporately.

Our solutions are often the problem, at the deepest level of our lives as well as in everyday experience. They hook us and those around us into vicious circles in which we get stuck. God intervenes at the point of our attempts at solutions, blocking them or letting them run away until they drive us to despair or kill us, or until by faith we do something different. God offers to displace them with life-giving feedback loops. The way God sets us free seems paradoxical, defies our usual logic, and often seems exceedingly foolish. We can learn a lot from God's foolishness.

Questions

1. How do systemic ideas and theology come together around the notions of paradox and counterparadox?

2. How does your congregation celebrate and embody the paradoxes that free us?

3. In the light of these paradoxes and of this book, are there any strategies for solutions you might consider now that you would have ruled out before?

Introduction: Free the Flow, Fan the Flame

1. Family therapy is a broad movement including a variety of approaches influenced by systems thinking. These approaches were developed largely by charismatic therapist/thinkers and their colleagues in the United States and around the world in reaction to the more individualistic psychotherapies that have dominated the mental health field. No one approach has yet been proved by research to work better than the others. Some efforts at integration have been attempted, and many therapists draw from more than one approach, but the strong theoretical distinctions among approaches parallel somewhat the distinctions among the theologies of various church denominations.

The Mental Research Institute (MRI) is distinguished by the larger variety of noted researchers and therapists, including Gregory Bateson, Don Jackson, Jay Haley, Virginia Satir, and Paul Watzlawick, who worked together to develop several related approaches to helping families. I find the Brief Therapy Model that came out of MRI particularly helpful for the part of leadership I call "freeing the flow."

I have attempted to incorporate emphases from other family therapy approaches to help prevent the model here from becoming too rigid, too problem-centered, or too technique-oriented and, at the same time, to help clarify true solutions. Much of what I draw from these other models, when used in the context of the MRI Model, is practical and fits well in the part of leadership I call "fanning the flame."

2. Peter Senge, *The Fifth Discipline: The Art and Practice of the Learning Organization* (New York: Doubleday, 1990).

Chapter 1: What Is Stuckness?
  1. Speed Leas and George Parsons, *Understanding Your Congregation as a System* (Washington, D.C.: The Alban Institute, 1993), 1.

Chapter 2: Is Your Congregation Stuck?
  1. M. Scott Peck, *The Different Drum: Community Making and Peace* (New York: Simon & Schuster, 1987), 86.
  2. Anne Wilson Schaef, *Beyond Science, Beyond Therapy: A New Model for Healing the Whole Person* (San Francisco: HarperSan Francisco, 1992).
  3. Paul Watzlawick, John Weakland, and Richard Fisch, *Change: Principles of Problem Formation and Problem Resolution* (New York: Norton, 1974), 38-39.
  4. William Easum, *Sacred Cows Make Gourmet Burgers* (Nashville: Abingdon, 1995), 9.
  5. R. Paul Stevens and Phil Collins, *The Equipping Pastor: A Systems Approach to Congregational Leadership* (Washington, D.C.: The Alban Institute, 1993), xiii.
  6. Stevens and Collins, *The Equipping Pastor,* xxi.
  7. Loren Mead, *The Once and Future Church* (Washington, D.C.: The Alban Institute, 1991).

Chapter 3: Systems Thinking
  1. Edwin Friedman, *Generation to Generation: Family Process in Church and Synagogue* (New York: Guilford Press, 1985); Peter Steinke, *How Your Church Family Works* (Washington, D.C.: The Alban Institute, 1993); Ronald Richardson, *Creating a Healthier Church: Family Systems Theory, Leadership, and Congregational Life* (Minneapolis: Fortress Press, 1996).
  2. This school was built on the theory of von Bertalanffy and Weiner. The MRI group was strongly influenced by the seminal ideas of anthropologist Gregory Bateson and clinician/schizophrenia researcher Donald Jackson. Paul Watzlawick and several of his colleagues added insights about language and logic from such philosophers as Alfred North Whitehead and Bertrand Russell and ideas from master hypnotherapist Milton Erickson, as they developed the MRI Brief Therapy approach.

Chapter 4: How We Turn Difficulties into Problems
    1 Watzlawick, Weakland, and Fisch, *Change.*
    2. Richard Fisch, John Weakland, and Lynn Segal, *Tactics of Change* (New York: Norton, 1982), 128.
    3. Ted Peters, *Sin: Radical Evil in Sou. and Society* (Grand Rapids: Wm. B. Eerdmans, 1994), 10-17.

Chapter 5: Paradox That Binds, Paradox That Frees
    1. Camillo Loriedo and Gaspare Vella, *Paradox and the Family System* (New York: Brunner/Mazel, 1992), 78.
    2. Loriedo and Vella, *Paradox,* 116.

Chapter 7: Mishandled Grief, Shame, and Change
    1. William Miller, *When Going to Pieces Holds You Together* (Minneapolis: Augsburg, 1972).
    2. Ivan Boszormenyi-Nagy and Geraldine Sparks, *Invisible Loyalties: Reciprocity in Intergenerational Family Therapy* (Hagerstown, Md.: Harper & Row, 1973).
    3. Evan Imber-Black and Janine Roberts, *Rituals for Our Times: Celebrating, Healing, and Changing Our Relationships* (New York: HarperCollins, 1992), 28.
    4. Senge, *The Fifth Discipline,* 61.
    5. Some family systems writers, such as Peter Steinke, have suggested that the main "virus" in emotional systems is anxiety and emotional reactivity. I agree partly, but I would add that the forms anxiety and emotional reactivity take, and the resultant danger, are often more subtle and complex than these words suggest. The more devious forms of mental pathology and evil may disguise themselves as "angels of light." Character pathologies and forms of evil may appear rational, calm, cool, and even charming, making those who become emotionally expressive look like the really dangerous ones when in fact the more dangerous rational, charming, but manipulation-and-domination-oriented virus stays hidden.
    6. Senge, *The Fifth Discipline,* 3.

Chapter 8: The MRI Brief Therapy Skills

1. Stephen Karpman, "Script Drama Analysis," *Transactional Analysis Bulletin*, 4, 26 (April 1968). This article discusses the Rescuer-Victim-Persecutor triangle now referred to in the literature as the Karpman Triangle.

2. Charles Cosgrove and Dennis Hatfield, *Church Conflict: The Hidden Systems Behind the Fights* (Nashville: Abingdon, 1994).

Chapter 10: Prevention of Stuckness

1. Stevens and Collins, *The Equipping Pastor.*

BIBLIOGRAPHY

Augsburger, David. *Caring Enough to Confront: The Love Fight*. Glendale, Calif.: Regal Books, 1974.

Bach, George, and Ronald Deutsch. *Stop! You're Driving Me Crazy*. New York: Berkley/Putnam, 1979.

Bach, George, and Herb Goldberg. *Creative Aggression: The Art of Assertive Living*. New York: Avon Books, 1974.

Barrett, William. *The Illusion of Technique: A Search for the Meaning of Life in a Technological Age*. London: William Kimber, 1979.

Boszormenyi-Nagy, Ivan, and Geraldine Spark. *Invisible Loyalties: Reciprocity in Intergenerational Family Therapy*. Hagerstown, Md.: Harper & Row, 1973.

Buckley, Walter. *Modern Systems Research for the Behavioral Scientist*. Chicago: Aldine, 1968.

Capps, Donald. *Reframing: A New Method in Pastoral Care*. Minneapolis: Fortress Press, 1990.

Capra, Fritjof. *The Turning Point: Science, Society, and the Rising Culture*. New York: Simon & Schuster, 1982.

Cosgrove, Charles, and Dennis Hatfield. *Church Conflict: The Hidden System Behind the Fights*. Nashville: Abingdon, 1994.

Creighton, James. *Don't Go Away Mad: How to Make Peace with Your Partner*. New York: Doubleday, 1989.

De Shazer, Steve. *Clues: Investigating Solutions in Brief Therapy*. New York: Norton, 1988.

————. *Keys to Solution in Brief Therapy*. New York: Norton, 1985.

————. *Putting Difference to Work*. New York: Norton, 1991.

Easum, William. *Sacred Cows Make Gourmet Burgers*. Nashville: Abingdon, 1995.

Elkaim, Mony. *If You Love Me, Don't Love Me: Undoing Reciprocal Double Binds and Other Methods of Change in Couple and Family Therapy.* Northvale, N.J.: Jason Aronson, 1990.

Fisch, Richard, John Weakland, and Lynn Segal. *Tactics of Change: Doing Therapy Briefly.* New York: Norton, 1982.

Fossum, Merle, and Marilyn Mason. *Facing Shame: Families in Recovery.* New York: Norton, 1986.

Fox, Matthew. *A Spirituality Named Compassion: And the Healing of the Global Village, Humpty Dumpty and Us.* Minneapolis: Winston Press, 1979.

Friedman, Edwin H. *Generation to Generation: Family Process in Church and Synagogue.* New York: Guilford Press, 1985.

Gill, Jerry. *On Knowing God: New Directions for the Future of Theology.* Philadelphia: Westminster, 1981.

Glasse, James D. *Putting It Together in the Parish.* Nashville: Abingdon, 1972.

Gurman, Alan S., and David P. Kniskern, eds. *Handbook of Family Therapy.* New York: Brunner/Mazel, 1981.

Hahn, Celia Allison. *Growing in Authority, Relinquishing Control: A New Approach to Faithful Leadership.* Bethesda, Md.: The Alban Institute, 1994.

Haley, Jay. *Uncommon Therapy: The Psychiatric Techniques of Milton H. Erickson, M.D.* New York: Norton, 1973.

————. *Problem-Solving Therapy: New Strategies for Effective Family Therapy.* New York: Harper & Row, 1976.

Haugk, Kenneth. *Antagonists in the Church.* Minneapolis: Augsburg, 1991.

Hoffman, Lynn. *Foundations of Family Therapy.* New York: Basic Books, 1981.

Kerr, Michael, and Murray Bowen. *Family Evaluation.* New York: W. W. Norton, 1988.

Krebs, Richard. *Creative Conflict.* Minneapolis: Augsburg, 1982.

Leas, Speed. *Leadership and Conflict.* Nashville: Abingdon, 1982.

Lerner, Harriet Goldhor. *The Dance of Anger: A Woman's Guide to Changing the Patterns of Intimate Relationships.* New York: Harper & Row, 1985.

Loriedo, Camillo, and Gaspare Vella. *Paradox and the Family System.* New York: Brunner/ Mazel, 1992.

Mead, Loren B. *Five Challenges for the Once and Future Church.*
Bethesda, Md.: The Alban Institute, 1996.

————. *The Once and Future Church: Reinventing the Congregation for a New Mission Frontier.* Washington, D.C.: The Alban Institute, 1991.

————. *Transforming Congregations for the Future.* Bethesda, Md.: The Alban Institute, 1994.

Miller, William A. *Make Friends with Your Shadow.* Minneapolis: Augsburg, 1981.

————. *When Going to Pieces Holds You Together.* Minneapolis: Augsburg, 1978.

Mitchell, Kenneth R., and Herbert Anderson. *All Our Losses, All Our Griefs: Resources for Pastoral Care.* Philadelphia: Westminster Press, 1983.

Olsen, Charles M. *Transforming Church Boards into Communities of Spiritual Leaders.* Bethesda, Md.: The Alban Institute, 1995.

Parsons, George, and Speed Leas. *Understanding Your Congregation as a System.* Washington, D.C.: The Alban Institute, 1993.

Peck, M. Scott. *The Different Drum: Community Making and Peace.* New York: Simon & Schuster, 1987.

Peters, Ted. *Sin: Radical Evil in Soul and Society.* Grand Rapids: Wm. B. Eerdmans, 1994.

Peters, Tom. *Liberation Management: Necessary Disorganization for the Nanosecond Nineties.* New York: Alfred A. Knopf, 1992.

————. *Thriving on Chaos.* New York: Alfred A. Knopf, 1990.

Pincus, Lilly. *Death and the Family: The Importance of Mourning.* New York: Random House, 1974.

Prigogine, Ilya, and Isabelle Stengers. *Order Out of Chaos: Man's New Dialogue with Nature.* Boulder: Shambala, 1984.

Qualben, James. *Peace in the Parish: How to Use Conflict Redemption: Principles and Practice.* San Antonio, Texas: LangMarc Publishing, 1991.

Rediger, G. Lloyd. *Clergy Killers.* Minneapolis: Logos, 1997.

Richardson, Ronald W. *Creating a Healthier Church: Family Systems Theory, Leadership, and Congregational Life.* Minneapolis: Fortress Press, 1996.

Rohrer, Norman, and Philip S. Sutherland. *Facing Anger: How to Turn Life's Most Troublesome Emotion into a Personal Asset.* Minneapolis: Augsburg, 1981.

Russell, Letty. *Church in the Round: Feminist Interpretation of the Church.* Louisville: Westminster/John Knox, 1993.

Schaef, Anne Wilson. *Beyond Science, Beyond Therapy: A New Model for Healing the Whole Person.* San Francisco: Harper & Row, 1992.

Schaef, Anne Wilson, and Diane Fassel. *The Addictive Organization.* San Francisco: Harper & Row, 1988.

Senge, Peter. *The Fifth Discipline: The Practice and Art of the Learning Organization.* New York: Doubleday, 1990.

Shawchuck, Norman, and Roger Heuser. *Managing the Congregation: Building Effective Systems to Serve People.* Nashville: Abingdon, 1996.

Steinke, Peter. *Healthy Congregations: A Systems Approach.* Bethesda, Md: The Alban Institute, 1996.

———. *How Your Church Family Works: Understanding Congregations as Emotional Systems.* Washington, D.C.: The Alban Institute, 1993.

Stevens, R. Paul, and Phil Collins. *The Equipping Pastor: A Systems Approach to Congregational Leadership.* Washington, D.C.: The Alban Institute, 1993.

Toffler, Alvin. *The Third Wave.* New York: William Morrow & Co., 1980.

Ury, William. *Getting Past No: Negotiation with Difficult People.* New York: Bantam Books, 1991.

Wachtel, Ben, and Ted Wachtel, eds. *Real Justice Training: Coordinating Family Group Conferences.* Pipersville, Pa.: Piper's Press, 1995.

Watzlawick, Paul. *How Real Is Real? Confusion, Disinformation, Communication.* New York: Random House, 1976.

———. *The Language of Change: Elements of Therapeutic Communication.* New York: Basic Books, 1978.

Watzlawick, Paul, Janet Beavin, and Don Jackson. *Pragmatics of Human Communication: A Study of Interactional Patterns, Pathologies, and Paradoxes.* New York: Norton, 1967.

Watzlawick, Paul, and John Weakland, eds. *The Interactional View: Studies at the Mental Research Institute, Palo Alto, 1965-74.* New York: Norton, 1977.

Watzlawick, Paul, John Weakland, and Richard Fisch. *Change: Principles of Problem Formation and Problem Resolution.* New York: Norton, 1974.

Weeks, Gerald R., and Luciano L'Abate. *Paradoxical Psychotherapy: Theory and Practice with Individuals, Couples, and Families.* New York: Brunner/Mazel, 1982.

Weiner-Davis, Michelle. *Divorce Busting: A Revolutionary and Rapid Program for Staying Together.* New York: Summit Books, 1992.

White, Michael, and David Epston. *Narrative Means to Therapeutic Ends.* New York: Norton, 1990.

Whitehead, James D., and Evelyn Eaton Whitehead. *The Promise of Partnership: A Model for Collaborative Ministry.* San Francisco: HarperSanFrancisco, 1993.

Willimon, William. *Preaching about Conflict in the Local Church.* Philadelphia: Westminster, 1987.

Wink, Walter. *Engaging the Powers: Discernment and Resistance in a World of Domination.* Minneapolis: Fortress Press, 1991.

Wyckoff, Hogie, ed. *Love, Therapy and Politics: Issues in Radical Therapy—The First Year.* New York: Grove Press, 1976.